Between Two Worlds

Between Two Worlds

Miriam Tlali

broadview press

National Library of Canada Cataloguing in Publication

Tlali, Miriam
    Between two worlds / Miriam Tlali.
Previously published under the title: Muriel at Metropolitan.
ISBN 1-55111-605-7

    I. Title.

PZ7.T584Be 2004   823   C2003907162-6

Broadview Press Ltd. is an independent, international publishing house, incorporated in 1985. Broadview believes in shared ownership, both with its employees and with the general public; since the year 2000 Broadview shares have traded publicly on the Toronto Venture Exchange under the symbol BDP.

We welcome comments and suggestions regarding any aspect of our publications–please feel free to contact us at the addresses below or at broadview@broadviewpress.com.

North America
PO Box 1243, Peterborough, Ontario, Canada K9J 7H5
3576 California Road, Orchard Park, NY, USA 14127
Tel: (705) 743-8990; Fax: (705) 743-8353
email: customerservice@broadviewpress.com

UK, Ireland, and continental Europe
NBN Plymbridge
Estover Road, Plymouth PL6 7PY
Tel: + 44 (0) 1752 202301; Fax: + 44 (0) 1752 202331
Fax Order Line: + 44 (0) 1752 202333
Customer Service: cservs@nbnplymbridge.com
Orders: orders@nbnplymbridge.com

Australia and New Zealand
UNIREPS, University of New South Wales
Sydney, NSW, 2052
Tel: 61 2 9664 0999; Fax: 61 2 9664 5420
email: info.press@unsw.edu.au

www.broadviewpress.com

PRINTED IN CANADA

This book is made of paper from well-managed FSC® - certified forests, recycled materials, and other controlled sources.

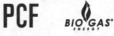

Contents

Introduction
My Background and
How I Began to Write

We were struggling. My mother-in-law had terminal cancer and she had suffered a stroke twice before we were removed from Western Native Township – our Thulandivil'e.

One day, when I returned from work, I found her seated flat on the ground on the bare step of my front door. The ambulance people had dumped her there, one of my neighbours explained. It was clear to me that I would *have* to leave my work and look after her. She was half-delirious and did not know what was happening. She could not speak. My husband was her only child; therefore, *I* had to look after her. The hospital would not keep her because she was, they said, "a hopeless case." The year was 1964 and apartheid was at its peak.

It was not only my mother-in-law I had to look after; there was my father-in-law who, although mobile and up-and-about, was elderly. In fact he was ten years older than her, well into his nineties. He was already weak and frail, having to rely on his "kirrie."

It was in the same year, 1964, that I started writing. I had left my work, yet I was not resigned to the fact that without my contribution to our meagre earnings, things would really be bad. That was when I thought of fighting the system with my pen – the only way I could. If I had not done that, I would have lost my senses. The days, months and years dragged on. In 1969, my mother-in-law passed away and I started looking for another job. I had kept working on the novel, whose pages

I had been hammering out laboriously on an old dilapidated "Remington" which I have kept to this day. But when I somehow completed the book it lay at the back of the dressing-table gathering dust. To me it did not matter anymore. What I knew was that I had done what I had wanted to do. I never really thought it would be published during my lifetime. I had accepted that I had written the book for posterity, for coming generations. I had tried several publishers and everybody had rejected it. The might of the Boers seemed quite invincible and there was no way we Blacks would ever break their strength. Amongst those I had approached was Longman Publishers, who had offices in Johannesburg. In desperation, I wrote a letter to Rev. Bishop Reeve of the South African Council of Churches and he replied, advising me to try Ravan Press, and I did. It was like a dream when I walked to their offices carrying the whole manuscript. At Ravan Press in Braamfontein, I spoke to Mike Kirkwood, a much younger man than the Director, Peter Randall. Mike Kirkwood later informed me that they liked the novel but … "it is too long." He added: "Publishing is an expensive exercise. We shall have to remove some parts." I objected and said: "But the book will no longer be the same!" And the man, stubborn as ever but smiling, concluded: "Go home and think about it." Some months later, they handed me the expurgated version. After I had read it, I was devastated and I sighed: "What have they done to you?" I looked at the pages as if this was a baby I had given birth to, now reduced to shreds.

I stopped going to the Ravan Press offices, and months later, I wrote to my mother. She took a copy of the manuscript, wrapped it in a spotlessly clean cloth I still have even today, and went to see a Bishop of the African Methodist Episcopal

Church (A.M.E.) in Lesotho. The kind African-American Bishop advised us to contact an African priest who was going to attend the church's Annual Conference in the U.S.A. When my mother called me and told me about what the Bishop had said, I was scared, thinking of what could happen. I selected a few chapters out of the book and handed them to the priest. He asked for a picture of mine and I wondered why. "They will want to see who wrote the book," he insisted. Later, my mother gave him a photograph of me.

Months went by after the priest had returned, yet there was still no reply from the 'Church Seniors' in America. I suspected that the priest had never presented the chapters to them. Yet another delegate who had also gone to America, told my mother in confidence that the lying priest was keeping my picture in his coat pocket all the time. We never heard anything from the American Church officials.

"Masolinyana [my African name], you better allow the South Africans to publish the book." I looked at her and shook my head emphatically: "No I will not do that, 'Mé, not the way *they* want it. It will only destroy it!" She looked at me and said sadly: "I have been waiting too long now. I shall soon die without seeing your book in print, my child." And *that* was the last straw.

My mother had raised me and my two elder sisters all alone. My father – a High School Principal – had died when I was an infant. Only my eldest sister could remember my father's face. I would never want to cause my mother more anxiety and disappointment.

When I arrived back in Johannesburg from Lesotho, I gave Ravan Press permission to publish their version of the book. I signed the contract. As if to add insult to injury, Mike

Kirkwood said: "Miriam, we shall also *have* to remove the title ... Why don't we just call it 'Miriam at Metropolitan?' ... *That* sounds nice, actually." And I objected: "No.... I will not have my name used like that!" The man again smiled and asked: "How about 'Muriel at Metropolitan' then?"

It was a far cry from "Between Two Worlds" – one of the tentative titles I had preferred. And I returned to my match-box house in Soweto, locked myself in my little bedroom and cried. I decided later to go away to Lesotho, when the book came out. I ran away. The book was finally published, or rather what was left of it. Five whole chapters had been removed; also paragraphs, phrases, and sentences. It was devastating, to say the least.

All that is now history. But I can never thank God for the fact that my mother was able to see the first book I wrote; that she was able to browse through it when I handed her one of the complimentary author copies. I can never forget the peace in her face when she kissed me because four months after that, she passed away. I buried her body with one of them.

Happily the expurgated material was restored when the novel was published in a new edition by Longman in 1979. "Between Two Worlds" has now been declared a classic. It has been translated into Dutch, Polish, German, French, and Japanese. I often wish that someone somewhere would offer to translate it into all the official (African) South African languages.

Between Two Worlds

Dedicated to

my mother Moleboheng

1
How it all began

THE BOSS came in, walking fast past the waiting customers to the other side of the counter behind the burly bespectacled white cashier, who was busy writing, receiving money through the steel bars and giving customers receipts. He asked the cashier, 'What's going on here, Pont? Why is the shop so full?'

'Bruce, there, is waiting for his commission,' replied Pont, pointing to a tall neatly-dressed African who stood leaning against an old radiogram, his arms folded. He seemed bored and tired, possibly of waiting. The cashier added, 'Those standing in a queue are waiting to pay. That one next to Bruce, with a cap in his hand, has been sent by Day-Nite Patrol. He's a night watch-boy. You asked them to send you one yesterday, remember? Those mine-boys there near Adam are refusing to pay. They say they want to see the boss.'

He pointed to three very dark-skinned, bushy-haired Africans who stood, also with their arms folded, staring blankly in front of them.

The boss removed his jacket and hung it on a stand next to the glass wall showcase, which stood behind a white woman with red hair. The customers waiting to pay gave way to him as he returned to this side of the counter, beckoning to the prospective nightwatchman.

'You. Come here, quick!' He sounded impatient.

'Bruce, ask this boy how much he earned where he comes from.'

'Five pounds a week,' Bruce said, interpreting.

'From what time to what time?'

'Five to five.'

'Tell him, I want him to be here from six in the evening to six in the morning. All right?'

'Yes.'

'You must be here every night. If I find you drunk, I'll throw you out. If I find you sleeping, you go. If you miss out one night, I chuck you out, and I don't pay you. Come, give me your pass!'

The boss held out his hand impatiently. The man quickly took out his pass from the inner pocket of his coat and gave it to him. Turning to a second white woman sitting on the other side of the iron bars, he said, 'Here, Lieda, here's his pass. Just check if it's all right and then we can send him to the Pass Office for registration.'

Again addressing the new nightwatchman, the boss said, 'You must be here at a quarter to six, eh?'

'How will he get to the Pass Office, Larry?' put in the woman called Lieda.

And Bruce, the interpreter, added, 'It's about three miles away.'

'Yes, it's a long way,' said the white woman, raising her eyebrows, 'and it will take him all day unless he is with a white person.'

The boss asked, 'Who shall we send? There's nobody here.

Lennie has gone out, but maybe he won't be long.' Looking at his wrist-watch, he said to the nightwatchman, 'Go and wait outside, I'll call you in later when the other boss comes.'

'And now, what do *you* want?' he said, pointing at the very dark-skinned Africans who were staring at him, morose and motionless. The one nearest to the boss was just about to say something when he was impatiently pushed away towards the extreme end of the L-shaped passage where an elderly African in a torn khaki dust-coat was sitting fiddling with a portable radio.

'Stand over there!'

The boss's eyes had focused on an approaching white couple, presumably customers.

'Can I help you?' he said, smiling.

'Yes, please,' replied the gentleman, also smiling. 'Can we have a look at your bedroom suites, please?'

'With pleasure. After you, madam.'

He led the way to where the bedroom suites were displayed. After about five minutes, the boss returned and addressing the red-haired woman behind the counter, said, 'Mrs. Stein, will you please attend to those customers? They want to buy a bedroom suite and they can't make up their minds. I just want to clear this shop a bit.'

He looked towards the corner where the three Africans were still standing, staring blankly and motionless. He approached them and asked each one in turn: 'What do *you* want, *you* and *you*?'

The one nearest to him mumbled something, and the boss cocked his ear, leaning slightly towards him. 'Hm, I can't hear. What did you say?'

He could not get anything out of them. They just stood

there at attention, motionless, staring. The boss shouted, 'Adam! Just get rid of these boys, man; they've been here too long, man. What are they all standing here and *katazing* (bothering) me for – what do they want?'

The elderly African in the soiled dust-coat answered:

'They want repair, baas. They don wan to pay six rands for repair, baas.'

He addressed one of them in Fanagalo. The man produced a piece of paper and handed it to the boss.

'Where's the radio? What has been done to it?'

'There, baas, on the table. Dire kod and new eriel.'

'Dial cord and a new aerial? Tell them they've *got* to pay six rands, Adam. Did you put in a new battery?'

'Yes, baas.'

'Well, I haven't even charged them for that, tell them.'

Adam explained to them in Fanagalo. They were still unyielding and the boss must have decided to tackle them himself. He said, '*Mangaki mali wena funa kipa?*' (How much do you want to pay?)

The men hesitated, looking at each other. The boss bargained, 'All right. *Mabili mapondo kuphela?*' (Two pounds only, then.)

The three men looked astonished; they looked at each other, their eyes widening, and shook their heads. The boss tried again. '*Mina haikona badalisa wena lo malahla.*' (I'm not charging you for the 'coal', meaning the battery.)

'*Serataputa, senhora, Miranda siranda – Wena lo-Portuguese eh? Wena lo Mashangaan?*' (Are you Portuguese? Are you Mashangaan?)

Everybody laughed. One of the so-called mine-boys, grinning, took out four rands from his trouser pocket and paid.

His companions were laughing, their gleaming white teeth contrasting sharply with their black faces. They were given a cash slip and left.

Some of the tension and anxiety I had felt seemed to have eased off. I was standing, waiting for my turn. I fumbled nervously for the letter my previous employer had given me. The burly cashier at the counter seemed suddenly to remember me. He pointed to me and said, 'Oh, Uncle Larry, that girl over there; she's the new typist. She's from the unemployment agency. She's got a letter from her previous employer. I told her to wait for you. Her name is Muriel.'

That was how it all started. How I took up a post at Metropolitan Radio, a retail shop dealing in radios, furniture, and household electrical appliances.

I had thought I had seen everything there is to see, heard everything there is to hear, in my experiences with people, black, white and brown, in this Republic of South Africa. But I was to realise that I had so far seen and heard very little of this beloved land of ours, especially as far as relationships between the different races are concerned.

I am no authority in the study of human behaviour. I do not profess great knowledge. I am not a writer. But I do not have to be any of these to know about Africans, their feelings, hopes, desires and aspirations. I have read a lot of trash by the so-called 'authorities' on the subject of the urban Africans – those who spend most of their lives with the whites in their business places and their homes; who travel with them day and night from place to place all over Southern Africa, who toil side by side with all the other races in all walks of life to make this country the paradise it is said to be.

The Republic of South Africa is a country divided into two

worlds. The one, a white world – rich, comfortable, for all practical purposes organised – a world in fear, armed to the teeth. The other, a black world; poor, pathetically neglected and disorganised – voiceless, oppressed, restless, confused and unarmed – a world in transition, irrevocably weaned from all tribal ties.

In the white world there are two main groups with two distinct cultures – the English-speaking and the Afrikaans-speaking groups. The former are aloof, indifferent, in favour of white domination. The Afrikaans-speaking groups are composed of whites of Dutch origin, who prefer to be called Afrikaners. These, boasting of political power earned through numerical superiority – are anti-African, anti-Semitic, and to a lesser degree, anti-English. They are despised by the English-speaking groups as well as by the other non-whites and Africans. In fact, all non-white groups look upon them as proud, arrogant, aggressive, ethnocentric and hypocritical.

The whites, with a few exceptions, are ignorant of the Africans' living conditions. This is partly due to their indifference and partly to their misconceptions. The Africans, on the other hand, know more about the whites because they *have* to know them in order to survive. With even fewer exceptions (in fact a very negligible proportion) their daily bread depends entirely on their going into the white homes, factories, garages, offices, or standing at their doorsteps looking for work, pleading or even begging. With the Africans it is a matter of life and death.

2
A feeling of insecurity

IT WAS arranged that I should come in on Saturdays for a trial period. As I did not work on Saturdays at Rand Bookkeepers, where I was still employed, the arrangement suited me. When I arrived on my first Saturday morning, Mr. Bloch, my new boss, looked around for a chair for me to sit on. He found one and pulled it forward, but just as I was about to sit down, he whipped the rubber cushion from its seat and, seemingly deep in thought, placed it against the glass show-case behind us.

On the following Monday when my former boss, Mr. Levenstein, asked me how I felt about my new job, I had nothing to complain about except that it was too noisy. Concentration was rather difficult with all the customers walking in and out, with the continuous clicking of coins at the till and the continual buzzing of the telephone, mingled with the endless noise from the keys of the office machines and the eager, loud, unmistakable voice of Adam. And from outside came the endless droning and hooting of the traffic. I was accustomed to the quiet, airy, book-keepers' office, high up on the eleventh floor of Helion House in Pritchard Street, where I sat alone for most hours of the day, answering telephone calls now and again. So I looked forward to coming back to my quiet office on the Monday morning.

But my movement from one place of employment to another could not go on forever. Mr. Levenstein had sold his business; my trial period was over, and I had to take up my post at Metropolitan Radio permanently. In my bag I had a testimonial from Mr. Levenstein. Not that it was much of a testimonial; he had conveniently omitted to mention that he had used me for two years as his senior balance sheet typist. He had had hundreds of clients, and the arrangement and layout, typing and binding of all the balance sheets was left entirely to me. But I was black, so he was not going to mention it; nor was he going to encourage his successor to pay me for my experience.

When I reported to Metropolitan Radio on my first weekday, I found my table and cushionless chair ready for me upstairs in a sort of enlarged attic, part of which was used as a workshop. The three radio mechanics – two whites and a Coloured – occupied places along a work table pushed against a wall and fitted with all kinds of gadgets, lamps, plugs, etc. On the plank floor next to the mechanics were arranged portable radios, portograms and radiograms of different sizes and makes, with a brown tag attached to each.

Douglas, the Coloured mechanic, was very friendly. It was from him that I learnt a lot about the place and its staff. The boss, Mr. Bloch, he said, was a kind man but unfortunately henpecked by the two middle-aged women, Mrs. Kuhn, the boss's sister, and Mrs. Stein.

'You would think Mrs. Kuhn owns the business, the way she pushes herself forward,' said Douglas. 'Mrs. Stein, the one with the red hair, has been with the firm for many years. She makes a point of remaining with the boss every evening long after everybody else has left, finding fault with everyone. She works for her good name! Then there's another white woman, a Miss Nel. She has gone on honeymoon. But she's the only one besides the boss and Ponty, the cashier, who speaks to you like you are a human being. You wouldn't say she is a Boer like Mrs. Stein and this fool here,' he added bitterly, pointing to the empty chair normally occupied by one of the white mechanics. 'His name is Lennie. They should have named him Stupid!'

I grew to like being in this elevated place. From there I could see clearly what was happening in the shop; who came in and who walked out. I noticed that besides the customers and the members of the staff and labourers, there also came in from time to time the postman, agents or salesmen, travellers – mainly whites representing firms all over the reef, beggars – black and white. From here, too, I could listen to the high-pitched voices of the white women downstairs enjoying a chat whenever the boss wasn't in. Even if I didn't actually see the boss walk out, I could easily tell from their voices that he was away.

'I expected them to object to you sitting down there with them,' said Douglas softly to me. 'I knew they'd do something about it. Now you've been tucked up here!'

'I don't mind, Douglas. I like it here. I like to be alone. Only I do not like those steep stairs. I feel nervous when I go down. And I like Mrs. Kuhn, she is always so friendly and kind. I think she likes me too. I don't know how Mrs. Stein feels about me, though; she never greets me when I greet her, and she sulks when I ask questions.'

'What do you expect?' said Douglas. 'She's a lousy Boer like this fool here.' He pointed to Lennie's empty chair.

'What about the other mechanic? He always greets me. Why aren't they here today?'

'You mean Peter. Oh, he's all right. He's a Jew too, a relative of Mr. Bloch's. He's not as stupid as the Boer. Of course he's still learning. They attend classes at the technical college once every week while they're apprentices. I don't know what they learn there because they come out of there just as dumb as they went in. Hey listen!'

I listened. It was Ponty speaking loudly on the telephone.

'Hmm ... Hmmm ... what did you say your name was? What? You want to know what is left in your F.M.? Didn't you get a statement? A statement ... a paper ... a letter! We send you a letter every month. That paper you used in your lavatory was the statement. What did you think it was? Yes?' Then turning to the white women, who were giggling uncontrollably, Ponty said, 'Listen to this, she says yes. She would say yes if I asked her to kiss my *tuchas*!* Oh, you're too stupid. Mrs. Stein, please take this call. I can't stand it. She's too stupid. Says yes to anything.' Then to himself he mumbled, 'Oh, no wonder I have an ulcer.'

I was employed as a helper, and I went on helping. As I mastered the easy tasks without any trouble, I was given more by degrees. Later I was to help to fill in particulars forms for hire purchase agreements where the customers were blacks, Coloureds and Indian. This was to remain my exclusive duty.

The two senior women tried to reserve certain jobs for themselves and to allocate the more mechanical ones to me, such as folding letters and statements and putting them into envelopes, and printing addresses on statements with the

---

* backside. (Yiddish)

addressograph machine. I would accomplish these in no time and find myself idling.

There were approximately 4,000 customers. The white staff could not cope with all the work requiring skill and thinking. I was there and I could do it. I had proved that I could type anything as well as they could, if not better. The boss was not blind to the fact, so he called upon me to do more and more of the seemingly complicated work. He was not going to employ someone else while I was there.

So my stay upstairs was short-lived. The new customers for whom I had to fill in forms were sometimes elderly and could not be expected to climb the stairs to my desk. So I had to come to them. Another thing was that at times I would be using the ledger or an invoice book upstairs and then one of the staff downstairs would need it and I would have to interrupt my work and take it down. It was all too cumbersome and awkward and a lot of time was wasted. So down I came with my desk, chair and all. Old furniture standing behind filing cabinets was moved; a more or less convenient place was created for me just below the stairs. I was separated from the rest of the white staff by the cabinets and steel mesh wires.

I had seen apartheid applied in many spheres in the Republic but never before had I seen it applied to ledger or record cards! At Metropolitan Radio we kept the European cards in one section separated from the non-European cards. It was all very confusing for a person who did not know the different Coloured townships because that was the only clue to where the card should be filed or found. The Coloured names were the same as the European ones. Inevitably a lot of misfiling occurred.

Then we had inside sales and outside sales. Inside sales were where the customers came into the shop to buy goods. Outside sales were for those customers who signed agreements outside the shop, that is, with the assistance of the agents or salesmen. There were six or more agents selling mostly in the suburbs to domestic servants living in the backyards of the white homes or at the top of blocks of flats – 'location in the sky'. These agents were each given a scooter and free petrol by the boss. As a rule they had to report every morning with whatever money they had collected and were given petrol slips with which they could have their scooter tanks filled at the garage. The salesmen who came frequently into the shop, sometimes bringing in new hire purchase agreements, were Abram, Silas, Hudson, Simon, William No. 1 and William No. 2.

William No. 2 was liked by all the white staff, who fondly referred to him as 'Little Wil'.

'He is as straight as a reed, that William. Never touches the boss's money,' Mrs. Kuhn would say, her voice ringing with sincerity. William No. 1 travelled in his own car – a huge blue American 'Biscayne'. He was as proud of his car as he was of the position he held as top salesman for Metropolitan Radio.

'I earn more money than any other salesman in this place,' he told me. 'You will be happy to work here if that red-haired Boer does not work you out of a job. With me she has failed. She's jealous of any good thing an African does. Fortunately the boss knows her and just pays lip service to what she says. Every month when I get the cheque for my commission and she sees the amount of money I earn, she feels like going to the lavatory to go and crap!'

'Do you have a lot of customers?' I asked.

'Hundreds! Haven't you seen my name on all the cards? Of course, maybe she won't even let you touch them; she's too jealous. I don't go in for small business like selling portable radios.

I sell big things like furniture, stoves, electrical appliances, and so on. But the only thing I am not happy about is the rate of interest at this place. It's killing our people. Every time I introduce a person here, I know he'll pay and pay and pay. It makes me feel guilty, like I've brought him to be slaughtered.'

'How are the other shops? Don't they also charge interest?'

"They do. But not as high as here. You'll see.'

William No. 1 went off to the stairs. I sat alone thinking and trembling. Suddenly I experienced a feeling of uneasiness and loneliness such as I had never known in a job before. I felt hopeless. How was I going to work with people who were not even prepared to give me a chance and who were squeezing as much money as they could out of my own black fellow workers?

3
The boss

THERE WAS no place quite like Metropolitan Radio. And Metropolitan Radio would not have had its unique character without its sole proprietor, the unpredictable Mr. Bloch, undoubtedly the most eccentric character I have ever met.

'I am over forty years in this business and I have never had a partner,' the boss boasted to a traveller one day.

The white assistants complained that of late Mr. Bloch had taken to grumbling. Once when Mrs. Kuhn, his sister, pointed that out, Mrs. Stein answered, 'I am not surprised, Mrs. Kuhn; how can he hope to do everything alone? Be manager, business consultant, salesman, clerk, all at the same time? And he is not growing any younger. His memory isn't so good any more.'

Ponty, the cashier, added, 'Yes, he has no manager. He uses Adam!'

Mr. Bloch did not employ shop salesmen, white or black. Of the white salesmen, he said, 'They just sit and gaze around. The next thing you have to pay them a lot of money.' Of the black ones, he said, 'They think they know a lot. But they are all liars and thieves!'

He was short and plump. He wore his clothes loosely. He

walked fast with his feet rather turned out, like Charlie Chaplin. When you looked at the back of his head, his grey hair looked like a horse-shoe with a bald circle at the crown of his head.

Mr. Bloch had no office of his own. This, I learnt from Adam, was by design. Having an office would restrict him to some secluded spot. That was not for him, Adam told me. He liked to be near to see and hear everything that went on.

One day I had been out for lunch and on my return I found him busy fiddling with the articles and papers on my desk. He was scrutinising every bit of paper. I just stood and looked on helplessly. The disgust I felt must have been reflected on my face because he turned to me and said apologetically, 'You see, Muriel, I must know everything that's going on.'

Then he blurted out, 'Muriel, why do you bring in such a big bag?'

I later complained to Adam that if that sort of thing went on I would resign; that I couldn't stand being watched all the time like a convict.

Adam in his wisdom laughed and said, 'Please, Muriel, just ignore him. He is a sick man. Don't you see him always look-ing at me suspiciously or hear him asking me what I'm carry-ing every afternoon when I go home with a parcel? How long have I been here?' Adam answered himself emphatically, 'I have worked for him faithfully for twenty-six years but he still doesn't trust me even for one second!'

Adam shook his head.

'He even says he doesn't trust himself! What can you do with a man like that?'

Yet of all the people at Metropolitan Radio, black and white, Adam was the only one Mr. Bloch trusted, a little, that is. If he was not in the shop, or if he had to go away somewhere, then Adam had to sit *on* the chair Mr. Bloch occupied and watch the door. Once I asked Adam why Mr. Bloch always asked him to sit and watch the door, and he said that he had to see what was coming into the shop and what was going out of it.

So Adam could never stay away from work. When he fell ill, which was only once in all the time I was at Metropolitan Radio, the boss told Mrs. Kuhn to phone his own physician.

'Don't call Dr. Schelling, Lieda, please,' he said.

'But why, Larry?' asked his sister, surprised. 'He has been your family doctor for years. Surely ...'

'He is a liar, like all doctors and lawyers! They are blood-suckers. For over twenty years he has been telling me that I have a weak heart. A weak heart, a weak heart, all the time. Now the other day, on Davie's advice, I went to see Dr. Linsk and he said it was not true. He's the only one I can trust now. Tell him to come to the shop as soon as he can, Lieda.'

When the doctor came, he examined Adam right there behind the wardrobes, administered injections, and prescribed medicines, after which Adam returned to his post as sentinel.

Mr. Bloch's knowledge of business methods and procedures was very extensive. But he made decisions irrespective of whether they were acceptable in bookkeeping or not. For example, he would pay out of his own pocket for certain minor purchases without putting it on record. Or he would take money out of the till and pay for things and not bother to make a note of it. This resulted in confusion and waste of time as the cashier would very often not be able to balance the cash for the day and would spend hours trying to trace the irregularity. He had also never overcome the habit of dealing in sterling instead of in rands.

You could never know with the boss. He could be very firm,

even hard as granite, but he could also be very soft and surprisingly lenient. Perhaps the best description of him was the one given by one of the cashiers: 'Mr. Bloch appears to be very tough on the outside, but inside he is soft. His bark is worse than his bite.'

One morning I walked in and saw Adam in the passage speaking to three black women. The boss was on the telephone so I did not bother to greet him. He interrupted his conversation to say, *'Wag'n bietjie.** Just hang on a bit, lady, please. Sh … sh … Adam, shut up there, man, you're making a noise!'

'I am serving custom, baas!' Adam shouted back.

'You can serve customers without making all that noise. Your *woice* is like … like thunder, man!'

I guessed that he must be in a bad mood. He continued with his telephone conversation.

'I am sorry I have delayed so much with the delivery. My boy hasn't turned up for a week now, the one who drives the big truck. You see, only the small van is doing the deliveries. We can't take your bedroom suite in that one as it might get scratched. He has been sick. If he doesn't turn up tomorrow, I'll engage another one. Please don't cancel the sale. Your goods will be delivered day after tomorrow, that's for certain. Thank you, ma'am.'

He hung up, mumbling to himself, 'This Agrippa is a waste of time, man.'

He was obviously worried about the absence of the driver.

Word must have spread that the Metropolitan Radio driver had not been coming to work for nearly two weeks and that the boss wanted to engage another one. Scores of drivers were roaming the streets looking for work. One who said that he was still employed at Nel's Rust Dairies, but had already given

---

* Wait a minute; wait a little. (Afrikaans)

notice to leave came in to try his luck. Mr. Bloch asked him, 'Why do you want to leave where you are working?'

'We do not agree about money.'

'Why not?'

'I been working there ten years and they don't give me no rise.'

'Do you like *phuza*?'*

The man shook his head.

'You don't take? Not even one bottle a day? You never make accident?'

The man shook his head again.

'You know how to repossess? Take the stuff back from the customers?'

'I can do it, but I never did it before. I drive a truck delivering milk.'

Henry, the other driver, who was standing next to the stair, said to me, in the vernacular, 'That will be that. He'll never hire somebody in Agrippa's place.'

And Adam, who had finished serving his customers and had come to listen, also repeated the question, 'Who will repossess?'

None of the clerical staff had come in yet. As I passed Mr. Bloch on my way to the kitchen to drink some water, he called to me, 'Muriel, just come here a moment, please.'

'Yes, Mr. Bloch?'

He moved towards the kitchen entrance and I followed him, wondering what was to happen to me. Was he going to ask me to make the tea? Anything could happen, you know, I thought. He spoke to me softly, 'Mrs. Stein and Mrs. Kuhn have complained to me that you have been using their toilet.'

---

* a drink, usually intoxicating. (Zulu or Xhosa)

'Yes, Mr. Bloch, I have.'

'Well, they don't like it.'

'I'm sorry. A day or two after I arrived here I asked Adam which toilet to use and he said I could use the ladies' toilet, Mr. Bloch.'

'Yes. Adam didn't know how they would feel. I am sorry about this, Muriel, but you see, we are not all alike. *I* don't mind, but some people *do*, you see.'

He looked sincere, and I couldn't help feeling touched.

'Yes, I know, Mr. Bloch, and I promise I will never use it again. I'm sorry ... I ...' Before I could say more, he continued, 'I'll fix up the toilet in the yard here any day now for you. It's quite all right except that the tank isn't working well. I'll call in the plumber to have a look at it. In the meantime ask Douglas to show you the one he's using until yours is ready.'

He looked sad, like a child who had taken a lot of punishment.

I understood the true position. I was sorry that I had not been warned about the white women's feelings earlier. I would have spared them all that inconvenience and ill-feeling. I did not want to impose myself where I was not wanted. Besides, I knew the laws of this country did not allow blacks and whites to share the same facilities, and I was not going to stage a one-woman protest against them. It had simply been a matter of habit because at my previous job the boss and all the other white staff and I had used the same toilet, and none of them had objected. But it seemed I had carried the idea of being accepted too far.

As if to save the boss from an embarrassing situation, Adam called, 'Baas, come make a receipt. The customer is in a hurry. He's going to work.'

As the boss walked to the counter, he recognised the customer and said, 'Oh, it's you, Capetown! You're still paying.

When are you going to get finished? When you bought this furniture I was still a young man, now look, I am old and grey, and you're still paying. You must get a *move* on and finish this account.'

That was Mr. Bloch. You couldn't help laughing when he was around, no matter how tense the atmosphere might be.

'All right, *madala*,'* Capetown said, laughing as he went out and putting the receipt in his pocket.

I was dusting the tidying my desk when he called me again. 'And Muriel, one other thing ... I would like you to help with putting statements into the ledger cards. Do you think you can do that?'

'Yes, Mr. Bloch, that should be easy,' I said with relief.

'When Mrs. Stein comes in, she'll tell you all about it. I'll clear up here somewhere for you,' he said, pointing to a desk near the switchboard.

I thought he might have forgotten whom he was speaking to, so to remind him I said, 'I can do that at my desk over there, Mr. Bloch.'

'You can't take the ledger cards to your desk. They are very important. They are the only record we have, and if anything happens to them, we're finished. Too many people come to your desk, agents, customers, the boys, everybody ... we don't want everybody peering into our records. When you have finished, you can go back to your desk that side.'

Henry said to me in vernacular, smiling scornfully, 'So you're going to sit with *them* now!'

'*Tula wena*!'† the boss said to him. He must have guessed what the driver had said. 'Go and do your work.'

---

* old man.

† Keep quiet, you!

I looked at the little space I was going to share with the unfriendly white staff. There was no proper office with convenient, modern, labour-saving, systematic methods of record-keeping. There were just piles and piles of papers, books, catalogues, stacks of folders and files containing invoices, statements, delivery-notes, hire purchase agreements, approved and pending approval, old and recent, lay about. In fact, everything you can think of. Things were just jumbled around on tables and desks – a continuous stretch of office records mingled with portables of every description labelled and unlabelled with service cards, some coming for repair, others going out, some re-possessed, others traded in. There were radio spare parts, tape recorders, irons, electric kettles, and so on.

Later, when everybody had come, I looked and wished the boss would give it another thought and change his mind. There were too many people moving or sitting in too small a space, and there was too much brushing against and bumping into one another. And yet I was to be accommodated there somewhere, somehow, because the boss could not risk having the ledger cards and other valuable documents on the other side of the 'line'.

And so I waited. For hours I had nothing to do. Later in the afternoon, I grew more and more restless, so I went and asked him if there was nothing I could do while waiting for the clearing to be done.

'Just wait, Muriel,' he said calmly. 'I'll empty the desk for you and you can sit there and do the work.'

I just had to wait. No-one else was allowed to touch those piles of papers. He alone could do it.

4

While the boss is away ...

IT WAS a quiet Thursday afternoon. A traveller walked in, put his case on the floor next to the counter and stood holding the shining steel bars over the counter with both hands and leaning his head on them. He was clean-shaven and neatly dressed in a safari suit. I noticed that his black hair was speckled with dandruff. He looked at the boss and smiled broadly.

'Good afternoon, Mr. Bloch.'

'Good afternoon. What can I do for you?'

'Buy.'

'Buy what?'

'Floor polishers, home appliances ...'

Mr. Bloch shook his head slowly.

'Car radios ...'

'What discounts?'

'Twenty-five.'

'No. That's no good. Supers give a third and twenty-five.'

The traveler, disappointed, nodded and sighed. Mr. Bloch continued, 'Come and see me some other time when you don't have the time.'

The traveller frowned, puzzled, then perhaps remembering

Mr. Bloch, smiled and picked up his case to go. Mr. Bloch joined him and together they moved towards the door.

'Business is quiet. Everybody is complaining,' the boss added.

Halfway along the passage the two men met an African beggar who stood facing them with both hands cupped ready to receive. The boss called to Ponty at the counter. 'Just give him something, Pont, please.'

After a while the boss returned, removed his jacket from the rack and put it on. He looked towards the door and said, 'It's too quiet, man. Like a cemetery. Too many shops dealing in the same business everywhere. At every corner there's a furniture shop. I must go to town. Adam, come!'

The boss signalled to Adam to sit on his chair, then he went out. Everybody thought he had gone, but he came back again. He passed hurriedly to the switchboard and dialled a number. He looked at two African 'boys' who were standing nearby ready to pay.

'Get rid of them quickly, Pont, they're smelling the shop out!'

He waved impatiently at them with one hand, the other still holding the receiver.

'They're engaged, Mrs. Stein, just keep dialling this number. As soon as you get through tell them I'll be about ten minutes late or so.'

He wrote the number down and left. The boss had finally gone. The rare occasion deserved to be celebrated. Both white and black members of staff relaxed. On the white side of the 'line' there was as usual a lot of talk with voices pitched a little louder than usual. Appetites also seemed to be whetted by the boss's absence.

'Johannes,' one yelled. 'Go and get me a cold drink and a cream cake.'

'Order me a toasted cheese too, Johannes, I'm so hungry, I could eat a horse!' cried another. 'I've been on strict diet for thirteen days and I lost only one and a half pounds. I sometimes wonder whether it's really worth it. Life is so short and then one still has to suffer!'

Johannes was just about to leave when the cold-drink-and-cream-cake one called him back, taking a packet out of her handbag.

'Oh, Johannes,' she said, 'go back to the chemist where you bought this lipstick yesterday and tell them the madam wants a shocking pink and not a rose colour like they gave you. *Shocking pink.* Now don't forget!'

'Shocking pink, yes Missus, shocking pink,' Johannes recited as he came towards me. Then reverting to the vernacular, he said: 'The things are all so spoilt. Sit on their backsides the whole day and call *Johannes, Johannes.* No wonder their husbands don't pay any *lobola** for them. They're worth nothing. Lazy!'

We both smiled.

'Would you like me to bring you anything from the shops, my child? Don't be afraid to send me.'

'No thanks, Johannes,' I said.

I was reluctant to send him. How could I? He was a man and I was a woman. According to our custom a woman does not send a man. We reserve a place, an elevated place, for our men.

---

* bride price; the groom's gift as 'thanks' to the bride's parents. (Nguni)

For the moment it was quiet. Then Mrs. Stein spoke up. 'Pont, did you hear what they said? They are expecting trouble soon.'

"Who?"

'Don't you ever read the papers?' Mrs. Stein and Mrs. Kuhn spoke almost in unison.

'You mean in South-West?'

'Yes,' retorted the two ladies, again simultaneously.

'There may be a war very soon,' warned Mrs. Stein darkly.

'What!'

'Well … fighting … or some trouble.'

'Oh, I thought you meant *war*. I don't think there'll be any trouble,' he replied almost absent-mindedly, his eyes returning to the door. He seemed bored by the whole conversation.

'They had a cabinet meeting last night about it. They are expecting something really serious. The whole world is against South Africa. The new African states and everybody,' moaned Mrs. Stein.

'Yes, but the whole thing rests with the Security Council. Not the new African states.'

'Don't you know they took another vote?' Mrs. Stein insisted. She was now quite excited, standing and fumbling among the papers on her desk. When she failed to find what she wanted, she became angry and began to shout.

'Where's the *Mail*? Adam! Where's the paper? Don't stand there looking at me. Don't pretend you don't know where it is!'

'What, missus?'

'The paper!' she screamed.

Adam was in the habit of 'stealing' the paper whenever he could lay his hands on it. Then he would sit in a corner out of sight. He would read for a long time quietly studying the columns on horse racing. You could do anything with the morning paper, as long as you spared him the page with the 'tote'.

He slouched smiling to his favourite relaxation spot behind the long linoleum squares to retrieve the paper. Mrs. Stein grabbed it from him with a click of the tongue. She started reading loudly to the others, her voice tight with anxiety.

When she had finished, Ponty remarked, 'These black leaders with their eloquence and boastfulness, what can they do? They arrive at nothing, achieve nothing. You know in one of those countries, I don't remember which, I heard they had a table in their Parliament or something. Then instead of doing real work, they sat and argued about who's going to sit at the head of the table. So finally, after two weeks, they decided to get a round table instead of a square one.'

They all laughed. Agrippa, who had come to sit next to the cabinets near me, turned to me.

'Are you listening, my sister?'

He pointed to an African woman who had come in with a white baby strapped to her back tightly in African fashion.

'No, I'm not listening to you, Agrippa. The conversation on the other side is more interesting.'

'Yes, I can see that. You are on this side with us, but your ears are on the other side, with the whites.'

Most Africans rarely listen when Europeans or whites speak among themselves. They have learnt to live in their own world.

'What are you saying, Agrippa?' I asked, wishing that he would leave me alone.

'I was just asking this woman why she gave birth to a white child when she is black.'

The woman looked abashed. She quickly looked around

to see who was listening. She tried to explain. 'No, this is not *my* child, it's my missus' child.'

Agrippa ignored the explanation and added, 'That's the trouble with you women. We allow you to come into the towns and work. The next thing you bring us babies with hair like that of the mane of a horse, and blue eyes. There is only one woman I can really trust, and that is my mother. In this work of repossessing that I do, my sister, there are many temptations. In most cases when I call at a house to repossess goods, the woman cries and begs me to leave her furniture, and asks me not to disgrace her in front of her neighbours. In some cases where the husband is not present, she will even push me into her bedroom and offer to sleep with me rather than lose her goods. It's pathetic.'

'What do you do in cases like that, Agrippa?'

'I am Mlambo's son. I never yield to the temptations of any woman. When I do my work, I do my work. Where has the boss gone anyway?' he added. 'That laughing and yapping won't stop unless he comes in.'

He looked at the women on the other side. I was sorry I had missed all the discussion on South-West Africa.

'And then there was also another one of those black states where a cousin of one of the cabinet ministers who was put in charge of something or other went and bought a golden bed costing thousands of rands. So later he was chucked out because the people were starving while he was sleeping with his wife on a golden bed,' Mrs. Stein was saying.

They all laughed, except Mrs. Kuhn who must have decided to go on with her posting on the Burroughs machine. She suddenly stopped and ran her fingers through her hair. Something had gone wrong. But we never heard what it was because just then Mr. Bloch walked in. He took a quick look around. Nobody looked at him. Suddenly everybody seemed to be engrossed in his or her work. It was a scene of quiet activity.

'Well, I liked it,' he said, looking at his nephew.

'Liked what?' his nephew asked.

'The new shop. I think the spot is the best I've seen so far. It's just at that busy area where the rank is. All the buses from Ferndale, Newclare, Albertville, and all the townships, near the Indian market. Every morning you see them coming in like bees from Westgate station also. That is where they all pass, hundreds of them!'

'Who?' asked the cashier.

'*Soggadikas*, blacks, I tell you there are hundreds of them passing there every minute of the day. And weekends. You can't even walk there. I've brought their books and we can have a look at them.'

'You've even taken their books already. And you haven't even got enough staff here!' Mrs. Stein said, smiling and looking at the others.

'It's the best shop so far. And at that price! I couldn't let that chance go. Lewis made me a special offer. Many other people wanted it, but he remembered me because I helped him out once.'

'But who'll manage that shop? And that area must be pretty bad. What about all the *tsotsis** moving around there?'

For the first time, Mrs. Green, who used to be Miss Nel, spoke up. 'I wouldn't be able to sit for even ten minutes in a shop like that.'

'Yes, but how have the other people been doing business there? We can do it too. I think with a strong boy like Joe to

_____
* young men, usually urban youngsters.

keep an eye at the door it shouldn't be difficult.'

'Who's Joe?' Mrs. Green asked.

'That tall hefty boy without teeth. He's always involved in some kind of fighting with the *tsotsis* at the location. I think he's just the right boy to keep at the door and scare them, I mean. I think ... Ponty, *you* can go over and manage things there. We can get you one or two more boys to help with the sales and the cleaning. Also you must have two honest boys to escort you when you take money to the bank or when you go home at night.'

'I suppose that's a promotion, Uncle Larry, but where are you going to get honest boys from? Adam is the only one we can trust so far,' he added. 'How much does Lewis want for the books?'

'Two shillings in the pound. And they don't have as many bad debts as we have here.'

Mr. Bloch called the tea-boy. 'Johannes! Go and fetch the two big books from my car outside and bring them to Baas Ponty.'

'Come, Agrippa,' he said, moving away, 'Let's go and see what you've got on the lorry. Come! Don't waste time.'

The driver followed the boss. On the way the boss stopped abruptly, his attention attracted by an open glass-shutter on a show-case.

'It must be *him* again?' he shouted. 'Adam, why do you leave this shelf open? I told you to shut it every time after you've sold a battery or a portable!' He looked at the shelf bearing the portables.

'What was here? What's missing here? Did you sell anything?' he asked, pointing to a clear rectangular spot on the dust-coated shelf.

'Yes, baas, to mine-boys. A Blaupunkt, three band Barracuda, baas.'

'How much deposit? Don't tell me you've let another monkey walk away with a brand-new portable for nothing again, Adam?'

It was Mrs. Stein who answered, after being quiet for a long time. 'It was a cash sale, Mr. Bloch.'

'Was it? How much did he sell it for this time?'

'Forty rands cash,' answered Mrs. Stein.

Mrs. Kuhn looked up and added, smiling, 'They'll give anything for a radio. They would rather go hungry and naked. As long as they have an F.M. they are satisfied.' She added, looking at me, 'Shame!'

5

Mixed encounters

ADAM KEPT on bringing customers to me, one after another. It was again the beginning of a new month, and I expected more to come. But for the time being it was rather quiet. I had just finished fixing up the last one, who had come to buy a portogram. He had made the boss's decision easier in his favour by adding four rands to the twenty rands he had given Adam earlier. I decided to go to the yard.

Ben, the flat-cleaner, greeted me loudly. He seemed very excited.

'What's all the excitement about, Ben?' I asked him.

'Look what I've got, money!' he said, emptying his trouser pockets to show me coins and crushed bank-notes which had been stuffed into them. I was surprised. I thought he had been gambling.

'What money is that?' I asked.

'It's mine,' he exclaimed, weighing the money in his palms.

'Yes, but where does it come from?'

'From my room.'

'What do you mean, from your room?'

'Don't you know that I hire out my room to people?'

'What people?'

'To couples, lovers, any two people who come to me look-ing for a place where they can hide and make love. I make more money for myself that way. They have already started booking for the week-ends. The compound and hostel people are my best customers. They come almost every day and they pay well.'

'How much do you charge them?'

'I only charge twenty-five cents per couple. I charge more for a white man and an African or Coloured woman.'

'Why?'

'Because Europeans have a lot of money, so I must charge them more. Besides, I have to help to get them black or Col-oured women.'

He went on to explain that with such mixed couples, the risk of getting arrested was greater. Most of those bookings were for after dark and the nightwatchman had to be on the alert, for which he had to be bribed. And the police-boy on patrol in that area had to be 'encouraged' to be friendly.

'Do you have many such mixed cases?'

'Oh yes!' Ben exclaimed. 'This Saturday night, for instance, the Marshall Square police sergeant is coming with Hazel.'

'Who's Hazel?'

'Don't you know her? The beautiful Beauty Queen who is always in the *World* and *Post* and the other papers!'

'No. I suppose I haven't noticed her.'

'He is always coming with her, and he gives me a lot of money. Ten rands per night. I don't mind. I give them the room and squeeze myself into the boiler-room or in the toilet.'

Only then did I remember that I had actually come out to the toilet, and became aware of the heavy stench which emanated from the stagnant urine on the floor of the toilet. It was filthy. It was open to anybody from the street. I had forgotten that I had resolved never to use it again. Being in there was like being in hell. As you sat (if you could summon enough courage to do so) holding your breath, drunken men of all races kept pushing the door open and peering in at you.

'Oh, Ben, that terrible smell! Why don't you use disinfectant or something?'

'I always use it. It doesn't help. It's because these men drink a lot of *Ndambula.*'

'What's that?'

'The kaffir beer which is brewed by the white people and is sold in cartons to our people,' he said, pointing to the many empty cartons which were scattered over the grass in the yard.

I felt sick and I immediately turned back. I went down to the park. It was two blocks down, and it cost me two cents in the slot every time, but at least it was locked and clean.

When I returned about half an hour later, the shop was in a turmoil. Adam's head was sticking out over the heads of the customers and he held his right arm high up, impatiently beckoning me as I entered the door.

'Hurry, hurry!' he shouted.

'What's wrong?' I asked as I walked past the lines of customers along the narrow L-shaped passage towards my desk. I could also hear the boss shouting anxiously somewhere inside a group of Africans although I could not see him.

'Where is Muriel?' he was shouting.

The customers were waiting and gazing about them. Impatience and anxiety were showing in their faces. Some were sitting on old chairs, others were leaning on the second-hand furniture. When he saw me, the boss said, 'This customer wants a three-foot bed. He is in a hurry. He wants to get back to work. Fix him up with an agreement quickly. There are ten others waiting to be fixed up,' he said, exaggerating. 'We've been looking for you. Where have you been?'

'I went down to the park, Mr. Bloch,' I said.

'What did you go there for?'

Before I could reply, Adam asked, 'Where else can she go, baas?'

The boss, understanding, kept quiet, perhaps remembering that he had not called the plumber to attend to the tank of the toilet he had promised to have fixed up for me. Later, after serving a white customer, he came over to inspect the H.P. agreement.

'Let's see the agreement, Muriel. Who is he?' And turning to the customer, he asked, 'A *three*-foot bed! Where will your wife sleep? On the floor? Are you married? I can give you a big bed and you can sleep with your wife.'

He looked at the amount given for deposit and asked:

'He's got twenty-four rands deposit?'

'Yes, Mr. Bloch, that's what Adam told me.'

He looked at the man's hands, and without saying anything, smiled and grabbed the bank-notes from them. He was in a better mood now, twisting the money in his fingers and moving towards the till without bothering to scrutinise the H.P. agreement.

'Make out a receipt for twenty-four rands, Mrs. Stein, please.'

I proceeded with my work, feeling happier too. He came back for more agreements, and bringing with him the booklet, containing the receipt for the twenty-four rands. He gave it to the customer, smiling and saying, 'Now you can go home with your wife and sit and wait for the lorry to bring your bed, and you can both sleep on it – if you *can*.'

He patted the customer on the back and the customer mumbled something. Mr. Bloch turned to me and asked, 'What did he say, Muriel?'

'He wants to know on what day you'll deliver the bed, Mr. Bloch. On what date.'

'Tell him I'll deliver it yesterday,' answered Mr. Bloch, smiling.

Everybody waiting, except Adam and myself, looked at the boss in amazement.

The customer asked, 'What? How can he deliver it yesterday?'

'That's right. Goodbye now!'

Adam consoled the obviously disturbed customer by saying, 'No, you can go home, my brother. The bed will be delivered in a day or two. He's only joking.'

6

Letters

MONTHLY LETTERS are an indispensable part of the hire purchase business. It seems that as soon as some customers have
been supplied with goods, they quickly forget their pledge to
pay every month.

All you have to do is give the *baas* a small cash deposit, or
in some cases, a trade-in in addition to the cash deposit, and
within a very short time you are a proud owner of a radio or a
beautiful piece of furniture. Some are so grateful to the kind
baas – who makes it possible for even the poorest to own something – that they never fail to pay the monthly instalment. But
others pay regularly for a few months, then when the novelty
of ownership has passed, they begin to scrutinise more closely
their monthly statements, and realise for the first time, and to
their disillusionment, that the stipulated time of one, two, or
three years is not as short as they imagined. Quite often they
come to enquire why it is that instead of the balance decreas-
ing, it seems to increase!

Others fail to pay for a month or two because they cannot
meet their monthly or weekly bill – after all it is not only the
instalment on the furniture, there is also that on the clothes

for the whole family and the school uniforms. The rent, train and bus fares, school fees, food – all these have to be paid from the meagre pay packet. Gradually the account falls into arrears. At times the arrears pile up until the stipulated time elapses, then the whole balance is in arrears and the customer is now in real trouble.

Every month thousands of printed circular letters are sent out. For instance, at Metropolitan Radio we had the '14-day', '5-day' and '3-day', 'Last Chance', 'Green Letter', 'Personal Summons' and finally the 'Summons'. When all these have failed to make the customer pay, then the driver is instructed to 'go and load on the goods' and bring them back – that is, in the case of blacks. Where the 'bad' customer is white, the account is handed over to solicitors, an attachment order is sought, a messenger of the court accompanies the lorry and the goods are repossessed.

To these general letters a few words, phrases or sentences are added to suit the particular cases of the individual customers. The wording becomes more severe as failure to pay continues. The letter must be able to exert just the right amount of pressure to produce the desired effect, namely inducing the customer to pay. In the case of blacks, the letters may be phrased in any way. And I noticed that at Metropolitan Radio, the letter-writer was given licence to deviate from the usual accepted business letter. Indeed some of them were personal, insulting, even abusive.

At Metropolitan Radio, who could be better suited to the role of 'letter-writer' than Mrs. Stein? She not only knew the particulars of the three thousand accounts (inside sales, outside sales and Europeans), but she also recognised the faces of most of the black and white customers and could tell their names just by looking at them. The blacks found it unusual for a white woman to take the trouble to remember their faces and their names, and actually commit to memory the difficult spellings of all the African names. The black salesmen and customers were so bewildered by the excellent memory of this good lady that they often praised her. Most, however, accorded the baffling memory to the fact that she was a 'typical Boer', and Boers, they knew, had an insatiable lust for persecuting blacks. This perfect efficiency was motivated by that unmistakable burning desire found in most Boers, that is, to sit on the necks of the blacks.

Often one would hear a black customer say, 'Of course these Boers are always envious when we buy better furniture than they do. They realise that even if they try to keep us down by not paying us anything when we work for them, we still try our best to buy good things. They feel that we are competing with them and they do not like it.'

And when they did reason like that, no amount of persuasion could make them see it differently!

7
Waiting

IT WAS drizzling softly outside. The first summer rains were imminent; at least so the weather bureau had predicted. Nobody complained. The rains were welcome as during the past three weeks it had been very hot, unbearably hot. The temperature had continued to rise. 'Thank God it will soon be cooler!' everybody sighed with relief.

Lebitso Pharahlahle, carrying a cumbersome roll of sacking under his arm, greeted me. He put the bundle on the floor next to my desk, and from his inner coat pocket, he took a letter and handed it to me.

'Whose letter is this?' I asked him, taking it.

'Mine,' he answered.

'Why are you giving it to me?'

'Because I want you to read it and explain to your boss what it says. I am tired of coming here talking about the same thing when I have paid my money.'

I could see he was furious, so I asked him to sit down while I read the letter. It was written in the vernacular and it was only after I had read it that I remembered the customer.

'It's informing you that they haven't received the dining-room suite yet,' I said.

'Yes, and how long is it since I finished paying for it?'

I remembered. He was a labourer who was working on contract for a building company. He had bought furniture from Metropolitan and arranged for it to be sent by rail to the Orange Free State. After he had finished paying, I was instructed to write down clearly on a card the name of the person to whom the goods were to be railed, and the station where they could be collected. He was then given a free battery for his portable radio – which he had also purchased from us – as was usually done in the case of good customers who had paid up in a relatively short time. Lebitso was then assured that within a week at the most, his wife would find the goods waiting to be collected at Senekal station. So he had instructed his wife to expect the goods and to arrange for their cartage from the station to the location.

He produced his receipt book with all his receipts in it. It was nearly six months since he had finished paying for the suite.

I referred him to Adam.

'Adam, hasn't this customer's furniture been sent away yet?'

'I don't know. I do not think so. You know, I feel ashamed. I never know what to say to customers. Mr. Bloch is really spiteful, man. I think he is now becoming too rich. Every time customers must have goods ultimately sent off, there must be a string of quarrels.'

'Why did you leave this matter for so long?' I asked the customer. 'You should have come to complain long ago.'

Adam answered, 'He *has* come here quite a number of times already and every time the boss told him that the goods had been railed.'

'Yes,' the customer agreed. 'I used to come once every month until three months ago. Our firm had moved to near Klerksdorp and it was too far for me to come. Now I've saved some money to fight this matter in court if he can't give me my money back. In fact I have brought some sacking here with me to wrap them up and send them to the Johannesburg station for railage *now*.'

'But Mr. Bloch has gone out and when he comes back I think he'll be too busy to speak to you.'

Lebitso was determined. He answered, 'I'm prepared to wait. I'll even sleep here if he doesn't talk to me. I'm tired.'

Adam looked at him and shook his head slowly. The cashier called, 'What's that boy waiting for, Adam, did he buy something?'

Adam explained why the customer was waiting. She said, 'All right, my boy, just sit and wait for the master.'

Also coming in one by one to lengthen the queue of hangers-on, were the outside agents or salesmen. They moved in on their noisy scooters and parked them outside on the pavement. Four of them now: Silas, Abram, Hudson and Simon. It was the day normally set aside for collecting their cheques. Agrippa was already sitting, smoking his cigarettes, next to Lebitso. He too would have to wait for Mr. Bloch to check the deliveries before he could leave. Lambert, who worked at the store, and was sometimes used as a clerk in the absence of the store-manager, was also told to wait for the boss. They were standing about, some of them leaning against old furniture, and engaged in quiet talk. William No. 2 came in last. With the load of portable radios he was carrying in both hands, he seemed even shorter than he actually was.

As soon as he appeared, Agrippa shouted, '*S'bona wena, we*

Matanzima! (We see thee, oh Matanzima!) Ever since this day dawned, I'm seeing a human being – a real one – for the first time, oh Matanzima!'

William No. 2 put the portables down, smiled and went nearer to Agrippa to shake his extended hand, saying loudly, '*Ewe, Sobhuza!*' (Yes, Sobhuza!)

All the others, looking at them and amused by the performance, laughed heartily. It was Lambert who remarked in ridicule, 'What's all this Sobhuza and Matanzima business? You are greeting Agrippa as if you are entering a *kraal** and dressed in *amabheshu*† making *bayete*‡ of the days of Shaka.'

I added, 'Yes, Agrippa should be sitting on a grass mat spread over a floor smeared with cow-dung, and you, William, should be carrying a skin shield and a spear instead of those portable radios.' The others laughed.

Adam, pointing at Lambert and myself, said, 'By the way, we have here Johannesburg born and bred ones, children of the houses with the numbers.'

'Yes, Adam,' said Agrippa. 'Lambert does not have a chief, he knows nothing about the real things a young man *should* know, and neither do most of you here.'

'Just what are those things anyway? Tell us,' Simon asked.

Adam explained. 'The correct way of greeting your elders and respectable people is one of them. Chiefs must be respected …'

Lambert cut him short. 'What is a chief anyway? In what way does his presence affect my life?'

---

* an indigenous African homestead, or a place where cattle or other live-stock are kept. (Afrikaans)
† the traditional garb, usually made from skin. (Nguni)
‡ salute.

Silas added, 'Yes, tell him, Lambert, our chiefs are our location superintendents, all of us here.'

Lambert went on, 'All of you are governed by the laws of the superintendents not the dummies you call chiefs. They too, Sobhuza and Matanzima and the rest, when they come here, they must be under the superintendents or the city councils – the white men.'

Agrippa refused to accept that. He boasted, 'Not *my* chief, not Sobhuza, King of the Swazis!'

'Well, yours too, Agrippa, to a certain extent,' Lambert said.

'How?' Agrippa asked, challenging Lambert and Silas.

'The greater part of your land is owned by the white man, is that not so?' Silas asked.

'Your own boss, Mr. Bloch, owns a *huge* farm there, does he not, and tell us who's the boss *there*, Sobhuza or Bloch? Who?'

They all laughed, and so did Lebitso Pharahlahle, who until then had been sitting morosely 'waiting for the master', as patiently as only an African can wait.

But Mrs. Kuhn was already complaining about the noise 'on the other side'. She called, 'Adam! You'd better go and watch the door.' And turning to the other two white women, said, 'The *noise* they can make, I can't take it, you know, Mrs. Stein, I can't concentrate!'

Adam, moving away slowly, asked the agents to move towards the far end, near his watch-post. Lambert had come to get the money to buy a screwdriver for the carpenter. He, too, had to wait for the boss. Watching me folding the statements, he asked, speaking softly, 'Why do you have to fold all those letters; can't they get someone else to do it?'

'They used to let Adam and Johannes do it, but the ladies complained that they were too slow.'

'It must be a terrible waste of time,' he said, taking one statement and helping me to fold, saying, 'I might just as well help you as I wait.'

'At the last place I used to work, we used to send them to a certain factory where they used machines. It was done in no time. I don't think Mr. Bloch would want to pay for that. He doesn't realise it costs more this way. Every month approximately four thousand to fold. I think it is a waste of manpower.'

'He wouldn't want to pay for anything if he could help it. I should know, after working for him for nearly eight years.'

Adam and Agrippa were still busy arguing about the chiefs, with Adam's voice still more audible than the rest. Lambert looked over at them. He said, 'It makes me sick, this antiquated nonsense of the chiefs in the towns here. Who needs a chief? If people want to have leaders or people who make regulations for them, then the people must choose those leaders. Besides, we are detribalised. Our fathers and our grandfathers had no links with their chiefs. Most of them don't even know where they came from.'

'Yes, we Africans are undergoing a change,' I replied. 'We are fast acquiring the white man's way of life – we *have* to in order to fit into this modern world. As different tribes in the past we had a few cultural differences, but these minor distinctions are a thing of the past. They may be put down on record and preserved, stored away in the museums and archives so that coming generations may read about them and know them, but they now belong to an age we shall never go back to, an age we *cannot* go back to whether we like it or not.'

'Exactly. In fact there are greater differences between the English-speaking and Afrikaans-speaking groups than there are among the African tribes,' Lambert pointed out. 'Incidentally, last month we had a city council policeman visiting our homes in the evening. He had a file and in it he had papers with lists of all the houses. Under each number, he had to fill in details of identity of each member of the family or tenants. The heading on the last column was "State Name of Chief". I looked at all the numbers, and under each one of them was written – "No Chief"!'

We both laughed.

William No. 2 had just left the group of agents and as he came towards us, I heard Silas say, 'He's the happiest man in South Africa. As long as he sells portables on 7 ½ % commission, and he pays his wife a visit once a year in the Transkei, he's happy.'

Lambert continued, 'The Nats divide us up into pieces for their own gain. They try to sow hatred.'

It was obvious that William wasn't listening to what Silas and the other agents were saying about him. He preferred to join us instead. He asked, 'What were you saying about nuts, Lambert?'

'Not nuts, man, Nats! The Nationalists. You people … the Nats throw a few breadcrumbs to you and you imagine you've got the whole loaf already. You speak of your Matanzimas as if they were Kaundas and Nyereres. Let me tell you one thing, from the Nats, you'll have to wait a long, long time – you'll have to wait until the end of time to get *half* a loaf, never mind a loaf of bread, that much I can promise you.'

The argument on the Nats and chiefs might have gone on and on if Mr. Bloch had not come in, followed by an African 'boy' to whom he signalled to step on this side of the counter, while he proceeded to the other. All those waiting, Lebitso and the five agents, Agrippa and Lambert, moved nearer the counter where they stood looking eagerly at the boss.

'Stand there!' Mr. Bloch ordered the 'boy' who stood erect with both arms behind his back, one hand holding a greasy cap. The boss turned to his sister and said, 'Lieda, I've brought in this new boy for Ponty's shop. He'll do the cleaning there. Just look at his pass and have his engagement fixed up.'

It was Lambert who broke the silence. 'They're going to be abolished.'

Everyone looked at him. What was he talking about?

'What?' the boss asked.

'The passes!' replied Lambert loudly.

All the Africans started giggling, with the exception of Lebitso, who did not seem to understand what the amusement was about. The boss, his white assistants and the white customers did not enjoy the 'joke' either. The boss looked at his sister and asked, 'What does he want here?'

Before she could answer, Lambert replied, 'I've only been waiting nearly two hours for money to buy a screwdriver, that's all.'

'Give him what he wants and let him go, Lieda, please. He's got a big mouth!' the boss said impatiently.

Lambert took the money Mrs. Kuhn put on the counter and went out, still laughing.

'What about *their* commissions, Mrs. Stein; have you worked them out already?' Mr. Bloch asked, pointing at the agents.

'I haven't had time yet, Mr. Bloch. I was doing the letters. You did say I must attend to them first, didn't you?'

'Of course, I had forgotten. Can you just leave the letters now, please, Mrs. Stein, and do the commissions, otherwise they will be standing on my head here.'

Mr. Bloch then went over to the salesmen, some of whom were shaking their heads in despair. After he had conferred with them, he gave them permission to 'sub' whatever advances of cash they might be in urgent need of. Only William No. 2 remained, writing out labels for the portable radios he had brought in to be repaired.

Mr. Bloch sat on his chair sipping his afternoon tea slowly. Suddenly he noticed Lebitso.

'What's that boy still hanging around for, Adam?'

Before Adam could reply, Lebitso snapped out, 'I want you to give me my furniture and I'll send it off myself.'

The boss looked at the customer but did not seem to take him seriously. It was as if he was thinking of something else. Adam leaned over the steel railings and said, 'The custom wants his money back, baas.'

'Tell him to go home. We'll rail the goods. What does he want to do? He can't take them and post them now. It's a big job to crate the goods and send them away. What does he think? Does he think it's like eating mealie pap?'

The customer answered, 'But you'll never send them. I've waited so long. At home they've been travelling for miles to the station hoping to collect them. They've been spending money on hiring lorries to collect them. I want my money back. I'll go and buy elsewhere!'

'Go. I'll send them now because I can see you're cross with me.'

The customer was not listening. He was looking at Adam, speaking in vernacular and making threats. The boss asked, 'What's he saying, Adam?'

'He say he wanto tek you to kot fess, baas.'

'What, he wants to take me to court first? Well, let him go

59

to court.' And looking at the customer, the boss asked, 'Which court do you want to go to, the high court or the low court? There's two kinds of court, you know – the high one, and the low one.'

He was smiling, raising his arm and lowering it like a conductor before a choir, holding his pen like a baton.

The customer went out without speaking. I called him back to take his receipt book and the letter. He grabbed them from me and left, with his bundle of sacking under his arm.

'Dise no gudu, baas. You meke custom kros,' protested Adam.

'All right, Adam. We'll send the goods, first thing tomorrow morning. The next time he comes here he'll find the consignment note waiting for him. Lieda, please ring the store and tell Ticky to tell the carpenter to crate that eight-piece Manchester dining-room suite ready for railing tomorrow. Tell him it's urgent, eh?'

The boss took the delivery notes which were lying on the desk and called Agrippa and Adam.

'Come on Agrippa, don't sit like that. Go and get your boys and let them help Adam to load on that "Kaigo" kitchen scheme. Come on, Adam, quick. Agrippa, you've only got three deliveries to do this afternoon. You'll have enough time to do the repossessions tonight.'

The boss went out followed by Agrippa and Adam.

Mrs. Kuhn called out in a sweet motherly voice, 'Little Wil! Have you handed in your receipt book yet?'

William No. 2 opened his brief case, took out the receipt book and took it to her, and returned to my side of the 'line'.

'You know, I'm just thinking,' William No. 2 said to me.

'About what?'

'About what that group of agents was suggesting. They want us to make a sort of protest, something to make Mr. Bloch offer us more on commission and pay us more for repossessions and new business. They think I'm stupid. I may not be as educated as they are but I know how far to go. How can they ask for more when they are themselves not honest? In order to ask for more, you must show the white man that he can trust you. He is also a human being, he can think. When he sees you doing your best, he will give you more. I know their type. I used to work with such people at V.H.F. They used to repossess portables from some customers and sell them to other customers. One actually bought a car with stolen money and he used to laugh at me and boast that he was well off, that I would never get rich if I relied on being paid peanuts by the employer. Where is he today? He's rotting in gaol and that car of his has been repossessed by the garage where he bought it. I'm not going to join protests by mad people. I've come here to work for my wife and children and I don't want to land in gaol. The white man is the boss in this land, *he* is the one holding the gun. You *must* listen to him.'

And on that note, William No. 2 took his briefcase and hat and left. I remained alone, folding the statements. One with red print across it below the balance read: 'This account must be settled immediately without fail.' It was addressed to a Mr. Koos, Glenhazel – a European.

The boss returned from checking the goods for delivery outside. He went and sat on a chair next to Mrs. Stein and said, 'Now, let's see; where were we with those very bad ones, Mrs. Stein? Oh, I was still busy dictating a letter to you when we stopped. Let's continue "… We would like to advise you that …"'

And so the boss went on dictating the letters to the 'bad' European customers.

Another statement with red letters printed across it caught my eye. It read curtly: 'This account is simply rotten. Unless it is paid up as soon as possible, we shall definitely repossess our goods!' It was addressed to a Michael Tshabalala, Kwa-Xuma. There was no need to be polite to an African customer.

And on the other side, Mr. Bloch went on dictating loudly, '… Please bring down your arrears which now amount to R56.00 …'

I was thinking, 'William No. 2 is right, in a sense. They are crude; their grammar is bad; their spelling is even worse. But what does it matter? *They* have the say anyway, "they are holding the gun".'

8

The lorry-driver's trump card

WHY THE driver of the 8.05 a.m. Nancefield-Faraday train had decided to leave Nancefield that morning five minutes earlier, I shall never know. Most of the passengers walking towards the platform briskly but not rushing were disgusted. The trains had been late the previous week, and I had made up my mind to start the new month on a different note. I was sincerely disappointed because I did not want to let my employer down. I arrived at the shop about a quarter to nine.

Mr. Bloch was at the counter. A quick look around told me that Mrs. Green had not arrived yet. So that made two of us late.

'Johannes, has Adam arrived yet?' I asked anxiously.

'No. I haven't seen him. He must be late. It could be the Midway trains.' I sighed with relief.

Minutes later Adam slouched in, his 'Churchill' hat pulled over his eyebrows as usual and his knobkerrie in his hand.

'Mind the customers, Adam,' said Mr. Bloch. 'You come in walking like a bear and a whole hour late at that.'

'What can I do, baas? The trains!'

The telephone rang and Mr. Bloch answered it.

'Hello, … m … m … yes, Pont, I'll see. Oh man, you know, this Agrippa is a bloody nuisance, man. He hasn't even turned up yet, man, and I've promised people deliveries. He never does anything right. On Saturday he delivered a kitchen dresser and it was brought back this morning by Hendrik. The customer wouldn't take it. It was torn into two pieces. They must have been dead drunk by the time they delivered it and dropped it. I don't *want* him. He can take a walk, him and his drunken lorry-boys. I'm going to take my keys and lorry from him and "trow" him out! He should be in gaol, that boy, he's got a head like iron.'

He was throwing his right arm into the air, gesturing, and with his left hand holding the receiver onto his ear.

It was rumoured that the driver had borrowed money from a friend some time ago and had since then only been making promises that he would repay it. The friend had grown impatient, and had ultimately taken away the keys of his lorry. Fearing the boss's reaction, Agrippa had pleaded in vain with the friend to give him back the keys. In desperation, Agrippa started the lorry by connecting wires. He then drove all over the Soweto townships trying to raise the money to pay his debt. The rumours, passed by the lorry-boys who were with him during the unfortunate mishap, were circulated only among the black staff in whispers. Somehow, the boss and the white staff never got to hear anything.

The lorry-boys, who were sworn to secrecy by their 'boss-boy', reported on Monday for work. All they could tell the boss was that they did not know where the driver was. They had since then been coming to work every morning and helping Adam with the window-cleaning and dusting, or just idling.

On the third day of Agrippa's absence, I began to feel worried, wondering what would become of him and his job. When I asked Adam what he thought the boss would do, he just said, 'Nothing.'

'What do you mean, "Nothing"?' I asked.

'I mean he'll do nothing. He'll perhaps scold him and take off some of his money on Friday, that's all. Haven't you seen him do just that when Agrippa loafs on the other Mondays?'

'Yes, but this time it's *many* days. Besides, the lost lorry keys and the broken kitchen dresser … It's too much.'

Adam assured me, 'He can't do anything.'

'Why?'

'Who will repossess?'

'Can't he get somebody else to do it?'

'Do you think anybody will risk his life in the locations of Soweto just to recover a white man's goods?'

'Why does Agrippa do it?'

'Can't you see that he does not care about his own life, his wife or his children, nothing? As long as he gets money to drink he doesn't care. He's like a dead thing!'

I decided to erase Agrippa, his lorry-boys and their boss from my mind and get on with my work.

I looked at the calendar. It was exactly three months since I started working at Metropolitan Radio and I was still not sure whether I liked working there. As usual, at this time of the month, I was busy putting the statements into the ledger cards and of course I was occupying the desk on what I call the white side of the 'line'.

Of late, since Ponty had left to manage the new shop in town, Mrs. Green had got into the habit of indulging in light conversation with me. She asked me personal questions about my family, married life in general and she wanted to know more about our African customs. I would also help her with the spelling of some of the African surnames while she was issuing receipts. Some kind of uneasy, friendly relationship had developed between us. I got the impression that she was to a certain extent being ostracised by the other women. At times, when they spoke, she would make eyes at me. They rarely spoke to her in a friendly manner when they were both present, except to ask her questions about her work or give her instructions.

Mrs. Green and I were therefore both juniors, but because of the colour of my skin, I was the least. She had once said to me confidentially, 'Muriel, *luister altyd as hulle skinner van my. My man is al moeg van hierdie plek.*'* I was annoyed and felt like telling her I didn't like being used as a spy. At the same time I did not want to make an enemy of her. All I would do was to pass no information to or from any one of them. To me it mattered very little what they said about each other, anyway. I was there to do my work and I was not going to be involved in petty gossip.

This morning Mrs. Green had come in about fifteen minutes after Adam and had apologised to Mr. Bloch, who only nodded his head and said, 'Just hurry with those hire purchase agreements, Mrs. Green. They are urgent, you know.'

She sat at the counter next to me quietly typing the forms.

Some time in the afternoon, the telephone rang. Mrs. Green picked up the receiver and said, handing it over to the boss, 'It's Agrippa for you, Mr. Bloch.'

Mr. Bloch took it and listened. He took out a pen from his shirt pocket and, turning to Mrs. Green, said with a smile,

---

* 'Muriel, always listen when they backbite me (slander me behind my back). My husband is already tired of this place.'

'Just give me a piece of paper, Mrs. Green. I like the way he just says "send me two boys, baas, I want to load that Fireline stove" after staying away nearly four days. Where are you?' Mr. Bloch asked, speaking into the mouthpiece and writing. He replaced the receiver and called the mechanic upstairs.

'Lennie! Just take Long John and that new boy with the impossible name, the strong one, take them to this number here, 106, Q-o-d-a-s-h-e Street, Pimville. Agrippa needs help there. Take the keys for the small van.'

So Agrippa's orders were carried out. It seemed Adam was right after all.

And by the time the lorry-driver arrived, there was no quarrel and he wasn't kicked out. Agrippa had once more played his trump card.

When he appeared at the door, the boss shouted at him, 'Hei, *dronk lap*! What have you got on the lorry?'

'Five repossessions, baas.'

'What?' the boss asked.

Agrippa enumerated them proudly. 'One Fireline coal stove, eight-piece Paarl dining-room suite, six-piece kitchen scheme, one studio couch, one Supersonic radiogram, baas.'

'Let's go and see,' the boss said, and added, 'And how much money have you put into the right pocket and how much into the wrong pocket?'

'I only "sub" five rands, baas,' Agrippa said, following the boss out.

The lorry was fully loaded.

'He *must* always take the money,' said Mrs. Green.

'What did I tell you, Mrs. Kuhn?' Mrs. Stein said, looking at Mrs. Kuhn. 'Didn't he say he was going to sack him?'

'Well, you know *him*, Mrs. Stein. Do you remember what

he did to Abram when he said I stole his money? Nothing!'

I remembered the incident. Whenever she felt disappointed about the boss's lack of firmness in dealing with the black staff, she remembered how Abram, one of the 'outside' salesmen, had accused her of having counted the money he had brought in short by five rands. He had claimed that he had given her all the money. After a heated argument and swearing, Mrs. Kuhn had resorted to hysterical tears.

'Yes, I remember, Mrs. Kuhn,' Mrs. Stein said. 'If it had been anywhere else he would have been kicked out there and then. But what about when that fool Hudson said that I couldn't find his customers' cards because I was stupid, and actually said to my face that I should go back to school? And Mr. Bloch was right here and listening and he only drove him out of the office! Did Mr. Bloch do anything about it, did he?'

Mrs. Stein went on, 'I tell you, I was upset the whole day. I couldn't eat. It was my nerves, you see. I couldn't sleep either. I cried the whole night. And wasn't my husband furious! He said I must leave this place. Fancy, a stupid animal like that saying *I* should go back to school! A thing which can hardly write its own name correctly!' And she sighed.

Later, Agrippa asked me, 'My sister, what did they say about me during my absence?' (A question usually asked by people who labour under a feeling of guilt.)

'What do you think, after staying away for so long?' I said. 'Of course the boss said that he wasn't going to give you the receipt book any longer.'

'That doesn't scare me. You see, I know what the trouble is with him. He is influenced by those women. When I want anything from him I just wait until they are all gone. When they are not here, there's none of this nonsense. We get along smoothly together. How do you think I get him to give me money even when he has promised on his word before them that he'll never let me sub any more?'

'How did you get that lorry loaded full like that by yourself?' I asked.

Speaking slowly and boastfully, throwing his head back, he answered, 'I have Swazi royal blood in my veins. My name is Agrippa. I am Mlambo's son. And this is my work!'

9

A token of love

IT WAS eight-thirty on the dot when I arrived at the shop. Adam was already moving around with a feather duster and a dirty yellow cloth busy cleaning, and instead of responding when I greeted him, he pointed towards my desk and nodded. A man was sitting on a chair near my desk.

'Are you perhaps waiting for me? I asked.

'I think so. I was just told to wait for someone. I want to buy a radio for my wife. This is her pass.'

I looked at the pass casually and put it aside.

'I'll use *your* pass since you are buying in your name.'

From a pocket in his jacket, he took out a green book and handed it to me. There, written in bold red block letters, was *'PORTUGAL'.*

My thoughts immediately darted off, and I thought, the bold seal of colonialism – more of a curse to Africa and its peoples than it has ever been a blessing!

I took out a proposal particulars form from a drawer in a cabinet next to me and proceeded with the filling in, copying from the travel document and asking the customer questions where necessary:

1) Pass No. (I erased that and wrote in 'Nome Do Portado' Name of Bearer)

2) Full name: Cerveja Pindela

3) Address: Room 87, 'C' Compound (No. 5 Shaft), Crown Mines.

4) Do you share a house? Yes.

5) With whom? Room-mates.

6) Landlord: Crown Mines Ltd.

7) Previous address: Lourenço Marques, Portuguese East Africa.

8) By whom and where employed? Crown Mines Ltd.

9) Address: P.O. Box 102, Crown Mines.

10) How long there? 1 year 2 months.

11) Previous place of employment: Crown Mines Ltd.

12) Married or single?

'Are you married or not?' I asked him.

He answered, 'Yes, I am married. My wife, I left behind at home with my parents in Lourenço Marques.'

'But you said you were buying this portable for your wife and you gave me her pass. You also said that you sometimes sleep at the place where your wife is employed as a domestic servant, didn't you?'

'No. This one,' he said, pointing at the photo on the first passbook he gave me, 'is actually only my girl-friend. We have been together now for eleven years since I first came by contract to Johannesburg. We have children but we are not married. I pay my real wife a visit once a year when my contract expires.'

13) Occupation: Miner (I wrote 'Miner' although officially Africans are 'mine-boys' or mine-workers).

14) Age: 42 years. (Born ... In passport)
15) Trade references: nil.
16) Personal references:

I explained to the customer that it was essential for him to give me the names of two people, relatives or friends, and their correct addresses, preferably people resident in the locations in Johannesburg. The customer shook his head vigorously and said, 'I don't know anybody, I am employed in the mines and I never go to any of the locations.'

'Surely you know some of your "wife's" relatives? Don't you ever visit them?

'Why would I visit them? She is not my wife. I haven't paid any *lobola* for her.'

'You *must* think of somebody. Anyway, while you think, let's go on.'

17) Goods purchased:

Adam had removed a five-band 'Tempest' portable radio from the shelf, fitted in a battery and tested it. The customer liked it.

18) Cash price: R65.50 (As a rule, either Adam or Mr.
    Bloch gave the cash prices, no one else!)
19) Trade-in deposit: Nil
20) Cash deposit:

I asked Adam, 'How much has the customer given you for deposit?'

'Sixteen rands,' Adam answered.

'You know Mr. Bloch will not accept *that* as deposit because the customer is a mine-worker. You know he'll say he'll just disappear when his contract expires before he finishes paying for it. Besides, he has no personal references.'

Adam came over and asked the customer to think harder. He said, 'Try to think very hard, think of anyone. The baas won't give you the radio because your deposit is not enough.'

In order to help the customer, I wrote as reference No. 1, his girl-friend's name: Emily Tshabalala, c/o Mrs. J. Boxton, and the employer's address.

To be on the safe side, I also added her pass number: V/F (meaning: Vroumens/Female): 1846058.

Fortunately, her pass-book had the D/C (Domicile Check) stamp, which meant that she was registered, and that she was permitted to reside and work in Johannesburg as long as she worked for Mrs. Boxton.

In the blank space on top of the sheet on the righthand corner I wrote in boldly: Wrist No. C 7915. (Every African employed in the mines, wears, as a rule, a band round the wrist with a number engraved on it – possibly for identification. Nobody knew what it was called, so I decided to call it 'Wrist No.'). This number, Mr. Bloch insisted that we should always take to help us trace the customer in case we had to repossess any goods.

The customer was surprised by all the fuss. He said, 'I won't run away. I work in the mine and I am a police-boy.'

That would help, I thought, at least it gives the man some status. If the mine authorities could give him a job like that, it only meant he qualified, somehow, that he had certain qualities which distinguished him from the others so that he could be trusted and made responsible.

'Do you have any letter or something to prove that you are a policeman?' I asked him.

He fumbled in his inside coat pocket and handed me a white card:

CROWN MINES LIMITED
(Incorporated in the Republic of South Africa)
In terms Section 24(3) of Act No. 56 of 1955, as amended, I hereby authorise bearer
S/GUARD: N.C. 7915 GHONI CERVEJA

to arrest without warrant any person found committing an offence on the property of this mine.
Security Department, CROWN MINES LIMITED.
(Signed) Manager.

'Any person' caught my attention. It would have been more appropriate if it had read 'any non-white person' as, by convention, as well as by law, in the Republic of South Africa, no African or non-white constable may arrest a white person.

Under 'Occupation', I added, next to 'Miner' – 'Policeman'.

I then took the customer's travel document, the S/Guard card, the completed proposal particulars form, pinned to the hire purchase agreement form (both of them signed by the customer), and asked him to go with me over to the boss so that he could 'see what he looks like' as he always insisted, before he would give him the radio. I brought it to the notice of the boss that the customer was a mine-worker who came from Portuguese East Africa, that he had no relatives or friends in Johannesburg except his girl-friend, but that he was a 'police-boy' and he had his card to prove it.

'But where's the money for the licence?' asked the boss. 'You know, out of that eight pounds, I must take out two pounds fifteen shillings and buy you a licence. Your deposit is short; you should have given me ten pounds.'

I interpreted what the boss said.

'Tell him I'll come and pay again when my ticket gets full,' the customer pleaded, meaning when he had worked the required number of shifts, which took about five weeks.

The boss answered, 'After that you must come and pay every month. Do you understand that?'

'Yes, baas,' the customer agreed. Then Mr. Bloch said jokingly, as he always did with African customers, 'Raise your two fingers like this and swear: say, *"Nkos' Phezulu!"*'* he said, making a sign like you swear under oath.

The customer swore, laughing. Then the boss said, pointing at the customer, *'Pasop,*† eh, if you don't come and pay, I'll put *you* in gaol.'

The customer had passed the test.

After a receipt was made, the portable invoiced and the serial number noted, the customer signed the delivery note and Adam gave him the radio in a cardboard box. He happily bade Adam and myself farewell and departed.

He was satisfied. He had succeeded in buying a beautiful portable radio for his girl-friend, a present and a token of his love for a woman who was the mother of his illegitimate children. But one day his contract would expire for good and he would want to go back to his parents, his real wife and his

---

* by the gods, by the lord above. From *Nkos(i),* king or lord, and *Phezulu,* above or in the heavens.
† beware. (Afrikaans)

legitimate children, back to the country of his birth. So what then would happen to his other 'Johannesburg' children? For all I knew he was 'joined in holy matrimony' according to Christian rites to the woman in Portuguese East Africa, possibly in the Roman Catholic Church, yet forcibly separated from her by this cruel system.

It is a system based on cheap labour, which undermines all laws of morality and decency, making nonsense of the concept of the family unit. On it the mining industry in the Republic of South Africa has flourished. To my mind, it is comparable only with the slave trade.

10

A slap in the face

I HAVE COME to realise that the more you are ready to give, the less you are likely to receive. That people often take you for granted. That sooner or later you will be forced to demand what should have been given to you without persuasion. This rule (if I may call it that) holds for most commodities, material and abstract. But here I am referring to respect … You respect a 'white' person because he is a fellow human being and what do you get?

You always get brushed off, that is, if you do not land in the street or in gaol. After that, you get some 'respect' but it is of a grudging sort – always bordering on hatred. And always you will be tolerated rather than accepted; because you are an indispensable nuisance.

It goes something like this. You are standing next to a smartly-dressed white lady perhaps near a counter, both waiting to be served. She inadvertently drops something which you quickly rush to pick up and hand to her. She in turn grabs it from your hands without even thanking you. She may perhaps even give you a scornful look. You see, according to her, you picked up the article because it was your duty to do so and she does not have to be grateful to you. If you were daring enough, you might perhaps ask why she does not thank you, and very likely she would throw in your face, 'My girl, you must remember that I am white and you are black!' You suddenly realise that you should never have picked up the article. That if you had not, you would have spared yourself all the degradation, aggravation and humiliation, and that would serve as a lesson you would never forget, you tell yourself. But sooner or later, you find yourself 'respecting' again and extending your hand to help because you realise that it does not help to be bitter. You laugh at yourself and you shrug your shoulders. It is because you have been taught by your Christian mother to respect all humans. You slowly learn that not all Christian mothers teach respect; some teach that respect must be shown only after looking at the colour of the skin.

I had almost lost all hope. I had tried hard to hold on to my job. There had been moments when I had decided to give in, and I had contemplated leaving, but as usual, and typical of my old self, I had experienced a great deal of inertia. The idea of going about from place to place looking for a job had always been repugnant to me. I had been aware that I would have to work hard to keep my post, and God knows, I had tried. I was beginning to despair. What gnawed at me most was having to explain to the boss about one thing or another. Time and again – no matter how much I tried to avoid it – I would find myself standing before him to explain. Where would it all end? Those accusations which I always had to prove to be false. How long would the boss go on accepting my explanations? I was aware that he was receiving misleading and distorted reports about me and my ability as a worker.

I remembered the toilet incident, and the morning I walked in and greeted the boss and instead of responding he demanded to know why I had been interfering with the invoices in the basket on the desk he had allowed me to use. Of course I had not touched anything other than the documents I was working on, and had no knowledge of the invoices which were said to have disappeared.

Then there was the day when the boss sternly told me that if it took me two whole weeks to put addressed statements into ledger cards I would not do for the job. I pointed out that they had taken me only a few days, and that on the Monday of that same week, he had made me wait nearly all day for him to clear the desk for me. He nodded slowly and said, 'Oh yes, now I remember. Sorry, Muriel. All right, just go on with your work.'

And I should not easily forget how one afternoon Mrs. Stein had shouted from the other side of the 'line', 'Muriel, you claim to have worked in an office before and yet you do not seem to know what a legal document is!' I was confused and at the same time shocked to hear her address me. She had never spoken to me ever since I arrived six months ago. I felt even more embarrassed as her remark was made in front of customers, agents, and all members of the staff. What is more, I feared the impression it might give the boss.

I asked her, my heart pounding, 'Why do you say that, Mrs. Stein?' And she had replied, proudly and audibly enough for the benefit of everybody around, 'Why did you erase; don't you know that an H.P. agreement is a legal document, and that you may not erase anything you have typed on it?'

I was still confused. I did not remember having erased any of the agreements I had typed. I went over to see my 'error' and to her disappointment, I proved to her that it was Mrs.

Green, not I, who had typed the agreement. She did not even have the decency to apologise to me.

I was even more shocked the day Mrs. Kuhn grabbed the telephone receiver from me after the boss had called me to speak to an African customer as he could not understand what the customer was trying to say. The good lady had snatched the receiver and said to the boss, 'Larry, you made me sick. You're always calling "Muriel! Muriel!" all the time! Why do you let her speak on the phone when *we* are here?'

The boss immediately turned away without saying a word, and I left her to struggle with the African customer's broken English.

But perhaps the worst incident was the one in which I was accused of 'educating' African customers.

An African customer had come to me, after paying the balance of his account, and wanted to know about the interest charged. He had paid the whole hire purchase price, that is, the cash price plus interest for two years. But he had paid within eighteen months instead of the twenty-four months which was stipulated. He was therefore entitled to claim back the interest for the last six months. Or so I thought. I advised him to ask for a refund. He took his receipt book and a copy of his invoice and went back to the cashier. I went to the kitchen for my cup of tea.

The customer was refunded the money he had overpaid. I was surprised to find him still standing near my desk when I returned. He said he was waiting to thank me for my help. I politely told him that helping him was part of my job. He, however, insisted on leaving a ten-cent coin on my desk, saying, 'My sister, it is not polite to refuse anything offered in good spirit. Take that shilling and go and buy yourself a cake and have it with your tea, and may God bless you.' He left, and I took my empty cup back to the kitchen.

I only realised the gravity of the whole matter when I returned from the kitchen. I met the boss in the passage. He looked furiously at me. I was scared as I had never seen him look like that before. He said, 'Muriel, you take customers aside and ask them to claim monies they have already paid in so that they can give you part of it!"

I felt as though the boss had dealt me a slap in the face. Before I could find words to defend myself, he added, his eyes bloodshot, and the thick dewlap below his chin shiny with sweat, 'If you have such a big mouth, I shall not keep you here!'

'Mr. Bloch, are you accusing me of being a thief?' I said.

The sister stoked him even more, shouting, 'She can't talk to you like that, Larry. Let her go. Of course she sat there telling the customer all about interest!'

'He wanted to know,' I retorted.

'You did it because you wanted him to pay you!' she answered, screaming.

'If you really think I would do that in order to get ten cents your intention must be to insult me.'

I did not care whether the boss was listening or not. He had been breathing deeply with rage, and seemed rather surprised when I answered Mrs. Kuhn back. He stood listening to our heated exchange, looking from one to the other. Then he said, 'Keep quiet, Lieda, I'll deal with her!'

'Have you been telling Mr. Bloch lies about me?' I asked Mrs. Kuhn. She would have struck me if the boss had not stopped her. As she came storming towards me, the boss pushed her back, saying, 'Go back, Lieda. What's wrong with you? If she wants she can go, I can't pay her for telling customers nonsense!'

Turning to me, he said, 'You come here!' He led the way towards his other desk, the one he rarely used unless he wanted to talk so that people could not hear. He said, 'You say you will leave. Now let me tell you this, if you leave without my having discharged you, and without giving me notice, I shall not pay you your leave pay. I'll only pay you for the days you have worked this month.'

'Mr. Bloch, I never said that I wanted to go. It was Mrs. Kuhn who advised you to fire me and I answered her back by saying that I would rather go than be called a thief. Besides, I was never told not to tell the customers the truth. All I did was to explain to that man the implications of the hire purchase agreement, that's all, and I did that with a clear conscience, not aware that it was wrong.'

I was surprised that the boss had the patience to listen to me. Who was I, after all, what did I think I was? I kept expecting him to remind me as I had been so many times in my life, 'Don't forget that you are only a native, see?' But to my surprise, Mr. Bloch never uttered those words. He just sat there and listened to me.

At last he said, speaking softly, 'All right, I'll give you another chance, Muriel. But don't forget, you must have loyalty to the firm!'

And he said again, knocking softly with his fist on the desk, 'Everybody who works here must be loyal to the firm! Do you hear that now?'

'Yes, Mr. Bloch,' I answered meekly.

What next? I spent almost sleepless nights, just thinking of what might happen. I came to dread the very idea of going to work. So far, the red-haired Afrikaner, Mrs. Stein, had hardly uttered a word to me. She would only nod or shake her head like a mute whenever I asked her a question. I got the impression that she waged her fight through Mrs. Kuhn. She never risked a direct onslaught, she was too diplomatic for that. One look at Mrs. Kuhn told me that the war was not yet over; it made me shudder. Thanks to Adam's wisdom and moral support, I was able to drag on during this very trying period. Whenever I complained to him, he would calmly console me by saying, 'You just sit there and do your work, never mind those two women. This is not their shop. It is Baas Bloch's shop. You have already proved your value to him and he will never drive you away because of them.'

It was nearly five o'clock in the afternoon. The boss had removed his coat from the hanger, put it on and left. He had summoned Adam as usual to occupy his chair situated at the angle where the shorter and longer arms of the L-shaped passage meet – the strategic point, I used to call it. From there one could see almost every point in the large shop except the workshop above and perhaps the area behind the long linoleum squares where Adam used to sit facing the door, reading the horse-racing columns of the morning paper or just dozing.

The topic on the other side of the 'line' was Mrs. Green's stupidity. Mrs. Green had now left and been replaced by Mrs. Olivier. Mrs. Kuhn had been telling her how important it was for customers' names to be spelt correctly, that it would save the other members of the staff a lot of time when the receipts were posted onto the ledger cards and the statements.

'Mrs. Green was too stupid, Mrs. Kuhn,' put in Mrs. Stein. 'She not only spelt the Bantu names incorrectly, but also the English ones and some Afrikaans ones as well.'

'Oh, don't speak of her spelling! And her English was simply hopeless. Do you remember when she said she asked her husband to give her ten pounds to attend English lessons and her husband asked her how she thought she could learn English in ten lessons when the school could not "learn" her English in ten years! Well, did I laugh that day!'

Mrs. Stein went on to say that the English spoken by Afrikaans-speaking children was very bad. In *her* day the standard was much higher. Her neighbour's child, she noticed, was in the habit of translating too literally. She gave examples, and they all laughed.

There was so much laughter and talking that Adam must have thought that it was free-talking time. He came over to me. It was his intention, he told me, to slaughter a goat as a thanksgiving to the ancestors for his son's success at school. His son, Thabiso, was very clever, I learnt; he had retained his first position in class ever since he started attending school. I was just going to warn Adam to speak very softly – he was almost incapable of doing so – when I heard the white women break off their conversation abruptly. I thought it meant that Mr. Bloch had just walked in. Mrs. Kuhn shouted at the top of her voice, 'Shut up, you two!'

Then turning to Mrs. Stein, she said, 'I can't stand those voices! Those baboons there, sitting there talking.'

'But we are not making a noise, Mrs. Kuhn. Adam was just telling me ...' I tried to explain.

'Shut up,' she said! 'I don't care what he's telling you. And don't you dare to answer me back!'

'I'm just trying to explain that ...'

'What are you, after all?' the woman was now standing and glaring at me, shouting across the bars.

'What do you mean, what am I? I'm a human being, of course,' I said.

Just then, the boss walked in slowly, listening. He said nothing for a while. He just stood there looking at both of us, with his hands in his trouser pockets. His sister went on hurling insult after insult at Adam and me. Then the boss said, almost calmly, 'What's going on here?'

Nobody answered him. Still pointing at us, Mrs. Kuhn continued, 'I can't stand that girl. She and Adam are always sitting there and making a noise. No one can concentrate.'

Adam was also speaking, looking at the boss, and gesticulating, trying to explain what the cause of the trouble was.

'But *they* are the ones who are always making a noise,' I said. 'I only speak when I *have* to speak because she always insults me when she hears my voice.'

By now Mrs. Kuhn was quite hysterical. I thought she was going to jump at me through the rails. She was calling me by all the names she could think of. I felt that it was too much for me to take. Adam was also talking and the noise was intolerable. Mr. Bloch tried to take control.

'Adam, shut up, man. You talk too much!'

'Yes, that's her fault. She makes him cheeky like that. Ever since she came here you can't speak to any of them. She's always talking to all the agents, the customers, all the men.'

'But that is why I'm here, to speak to customers, agents and everybody who needs my help. What do you think I am, a doll or something?'

I had had enough of her insults. I took my handbag and was going to walk out, but Adam stood in front of me. He said quietly, 'What's wrong with you, Muriel? Just sit down and do your work. Just keep quiet and let her swear.'

Mrs. Kuhn was now panting and heaving with rage like a wounded tiger. Her brother was standing in front of her stopping her from dashing out. She said, 'Larry, if you don't kick her out then I'll go! Who does she think she is?'

I sat down quietly at my desk. It was a good thing there were no customers in the shop. Only the three mechanics upstairs were standing looking over the furniture which formed a screen on the edge of the plank 'floor' above. I thought it was the end, and I sat there listening to Mrs. Kuhn's ravings.

'Just because she knows a bit of English, she thinks she can say anything.'

I replied, coolly, 'Thank God I did not pick it up in *your* kitchen or backyard!'

Now that I was certainly going to be chucked out, I might as well let them know what I thought of them. I was going to force it down their throats and let it sink. I was going to let them have it!

Mrs. Kuhn turned to Mrs. Stein and said, 'She thinks she is like us, you know.'

I answered, 'That's an insult, Mrs. Kuhn. I don't think I'm like you. I don't *want* to be like you. I'm very proud of what I am. You're too small, too full of hatred. You're always preoccupied with issues that don't matter!'

It was almost quiet now. I was sitting and doing nothing. I thought I knew what was coming, and I thought with relief that I was ready to welcome it. It had to come some time, I had already resigned myself to the idea. It was nothing new. What was happening to me was happening to hundreds of others like me all over this country – victimisation and unconditional dismissal. It hangs like a dark cloud over the head of every non-white worker – no matter how hard you try to evade it. It is always there, it haunts you all your life – insecurity. There is nothing firm for you; nothing you can hold on to or fall back on. It is like that with everything you try to build up in every sphere of your life – your home, your work, your future, the future of your children – everything hangs on a thread. At any moment everything about you can be snapped off just like that. Your fate depends entirely on the whims of the white masters!

Any moment now I would be called to the office to produce my pass-book and be signed off and with that – unless I could find another job within a short time – would go my 'right to be in the magisterial area of Johannesburg for more than seventy-two hours', nor would I be 'entitled as of right' to remain with my husband for more than seventy-two hours. I remembered what my husband had once said to me, 'They are omnipotent; they have the power of life and death over us.'

I waited for the blow to fall. But what happened? Instead, minutes later, a customer came in to pay the balance of the deposit Mr. Bloch had required on the previous day. He brought the customer's receipt book to me and said, 'Just fix up this customer with an agreement, please, Muriel.'

I took out an H.P. agreement form and a particulars form from my drawer and started writing. I was still trembling and my hand shook but I went on doing my work.

If they are going to decide to let me stay, I thought, they'll have to respect me. Now that they know what I think about them, and that I can speak up if I like (and thank God that there is no law yet against speaking your mind to a 'white' person, or am I wrong?) they will have to be content with saying what they like about me behind my back as they do with other people, and not just blurt out any insult to my face at any time and in front of anybody.

It was twenty minutes past five. I started clearing my desk.

I was feeling uneasy and shaken. Instead of feeling relieved that I was given another chance, I felt disillusioned. I had not expected such insults from Mrs. Kuhn. She had always looked so kind and motherly. I remembered how she used to greet me with a smile every morning when I was still new there. It took me a long time to realise that her broad smile and hearty laughter did not necessarily mean that she was particularly friendly or amused. Somehow I was disappointed. I had made the mistake that thousands of Africans make every day. If I had been insulted and abused by, say, Mrs. Stein, it would have been easier for me to take it. You always know what to expect from the Boers.

At five-thirty, I took up my handbag to go home. I did not expect the boss to reply when I said, 'Good night, Mr. Bloch.' 'Good night, Muriel,' he replied. As if nothing had happened.

And Adam summed it all up, speaking seriously, 'I knew it would come to this one day. You see, if you hear a drum, made from the skin of a hare, sounding too loud, then you know it is about to tear!'

11

A lucrative proposition

'LENNIE! Where's Lennie, has he gone out again already?' the boss called out, pulling out the cuffs of his spotlessly white shirt from under his coat sleeves and straightening his tie below his thick double chin. I noticed the beautiful striking black cuff-links with shiny gold stripes to match the tie-pin. He was looking towards the workshop, asking the other two mechanics. Douglas replied, 'He's gone down to Gants for a cold drink, boss.'

The boss went back into the 'office,' shaking his head slowly and saying, 'Oh man, that Lennie, he's always moving around ...'

'He makes me sick,' said Mrs. Kuhn. 'I can't stand him. He can't repair a single radio properly.'

'Why, Lieda?'

'Because he can't repair Mrs. Miller's portable. He's had it opened up and lying dismantled on his table for nearly a week now. He can't finish it. He says he hasn't got the parts. Mrs. Miller has been ringing and coming in. When I asked him, he said he was tired of us Jewish people. I told him it's through the Jews that he's got food to eat. If it were not for us they would starve to death.'

Then the boss and his sister continued speaking in Yiddish.

After a while, the boss switched again to English to ask, 'And Mrs. Stein, where's she?'

'She said she was going to the C.N.A.'

'Has she started on the letters?'

'Not yet. Yesterday she was busy invoicing. Without the invoices the H.P.'s can't be sent out and there are hundreds already.'

Mrs. Stein came in carrying parcels and followed by Lennie. They were speaking in Afrikaans and smiling. Lennie was carrying a Pepsi-Cola bottle in one hand and he seemed to be in good spirits.

Just as the mechanic was about to climb the stairs, the boss said, 'Lennie, I'd like you to drive me to town quickly, please. Have your cold drink; I'll wait outside in the car for you.' Then, turning to his sister, he said, 'Lieda, I think you'd better come and sit here for a while until I get back. I'd like Mrs. Stein to start on the letters immediately. It's almost the end of the month now.'

'Larry, we must get somebody else, we're short-staffed. I have to do the books as well, you know, I've got a letter from the Bureau of static ... stactis ...' Mrs. Kuhn stammered and hesitated. She always had trouble in pronouncing 'statistics' properly. She went on, 'Well, those people in Pretoria and you know that *must* be done as soon as possible.'

But the boss left without saying anything in reply.

'You know, Mrs. Kuhn, Mr. Bloch really surprises me,' began Mrs. Stein.

'Why is that, Mrs. Stein?'

'Because he doesn't seem to see that we simply cannot cope with work. Yesterday I was doing the invoicing, and in exactly five minutes he asked me to do five different things. I was still invoicing and he called me to make out a receipt; while I was still doing that he said I must go and serve a customer. Before I could see to that, he said I must give an agent a petrol slip. Then he reminded me that Agrippa was still waiting for the "deliveries" to be made. Is it possible for one person to do all that at the same time? I've only got one pair of hands, I'm not an octopus.'

'Well, I don't know, Mrs. Stein, I really don't know,' answered Mrs. Kuhn with a sigh.

It was one of those quiet days again. Adam sat yawning on the stairs, looking out towards the door. I was surprised that it took so long for the women to start talking. Suddenly Mrs. Stein burst out laughing.

'What's the joke, Mrs. Stein?' asked Mrs. Kuhn.

'It's these letters, Mrs. Kuhn. Some of these natives really write the funniest things. This one writes: "I will pay my account next week Saturday. I have no money today. Because death took place. I am going to take some Body out of Muntuary. Yours faithfully, Jonas." Just like that. There's no address, no surname. How are we to know who that is?'

Mrs. Stein began to read out the letters, pointing out the grammatical and language irregularities and errors. 'This one just keeps writing letters in reply to ours. He just writes and writes but sends no money. I've got all his letters attached to the ledger card. This is the first letter – listen: "First of All I am letting you know that the end of February I am prepared to come pay my account for the Radio wich I fail to pay on th 1 of January I am well prepared to pay fast entill I get finish with my account.

    that is All Sir

        James Sithole

        110 mimosa Rd Northcliff No. 2"

Now the second letter:

"I am very pleased to Received your account wich you have send it to me and I know that I am Responseble because I fail to pay my account for 2 month and thise is all Ready the 3 month and I am well prepard to pay you the end of thise month to avoid the disappoint ment wich I did it and allso I will come and opologise to you because I know that thise is very bad Record against the law

from James Sithole."

Instead of paying, now he writes the third letter. Listen, Mrs. Kuhn.'

Although Mrs. Stein was reading the letters to Mrs. Kuhn, all the other members of the staff were now listening. Douglas had stopped repairing radios upstairs and was sitting on the stairs next to Adam and listening. Instead of laughing at the mistakes the two women were pointing out, he seemed to be getting annoyed. He kept remarking that *they* did not know so much themselves. We listened:

"'From today my new
Addresse is No. 360 Mimosa Road Northcliffe No. 2
I left at 110 Mimosa Rd on the 2 of October
I am now Bilongs to MR Mayers his full name is
Joseph and his full Addresse is No 360 Mimosa Rd
Northcliff
My full Name is James Sithole
Mr RevRence book No is 184976"

What do you think of that, Mrs. Kuhn? He says nothing about the money he still owes! All he wants us to know is that he now "Bilongs" to Mr. Joseph Mayers. How do you like that?'

Mrs. Kuhn answered, laughing, 'You must just send some-one out to go and repossess the radio, that's all. If he can't pay, then he must not listen to the radio. We don't want to know that he is receiving the letters and where he is. All we want is the money – tell him that, Mrs. Stein.'

'But Mrs. Kuhn, listen to this one, we must have it framed. It is simply priceless.

"Dear Sir,

Yours dated 17 may … , is to hand as dated above, with thanks.

In this note, in bold letters (LAST CHANCE); (FINAL WARNING) are written sir.

Personally sir, I wish to thank you for this letter, it is a very kind letter to me, the words in this note showed me that you do feel for me as your faithful custormer.

I wish to say once sir, thank you. May I say to you sir, I am done down by WILSON, Your collector. Seeing that he did not turn up to collect as usual, I wrote him a note and left it in his house door post box, calling him to call and collect.

Still WILSON did not turn up. I have even not received, statements from your acc. office sir. I am realy one of those custormers who never want his account to lack behind.

Please warn your AGENT WILSON to call at once to collect my fees. I can not give the money to any one else accept to him. His a-ction by failing to collect as arrnaged, puts a bad mark against my name to your fairm.

My name is an example to big firms sir, like for example, John Orrs, Russels etc. etc. from where I possess certificates of good customer.

I wish to keep my name up even to this your shop, to be able to buy from you even in any future sir or even to recommend my next friend or relative to you sir.

Please do not hand over my acc. to any of your lawyers. I do agree with you, in saying *Handing over such, will just cause every thing uneasy to me and even unpleasant for me and my family sir.*

Kindly send Wilson to call for collecting at his earliest, Tell him, I am very unhappy because by not collecting his firms money, he makes my name bad to you sir.

My Legal Advisors will not like this. I am ready with the money every second week of every month, he knows that, yet he fails to collect.

NOTE – Here Wilson comes in. I then told him all what I say to you in my letter in reply to you sir. I asked him to report to you sir with pleasure and to thank you.

Thank you sir once more,

Goodbye, Your Custormer,

........................"

'What do you think of that, Mrs. Kuhn?'

'I think he must be working for lawyers, Mrs. Stein. He seems to like talking a lot and showing off, don't you think so?'

The two women were laughing so loudly that they did not hear Douglas say angrily, 'They make me *sick*. Can't they find other ways of amusing themselves than by using the customers' letters? They can't even speak perfect English themselves but they point out faults in others!'

It was nearly lunch time. Douglas was again standing at the top of the stairs, doing nothing and apparently oblivious of his surroundings. He did not even notice Peter who was crouching next to him with a screwdriver in his left hand.

'Adam!' Peter called the elderly African, who was moving around the shop and keeping his eyes on the door.

'Yes, Baas Peter?' Adam answered.

'Here's your screwdriver. All right, don't come up. Just stand down there, I'll throw it. Catch!'

Adam came nearer, moving quickly. Like everybody else, agents, labourers, drivers, in fact all the staff and customers, black and white, Adam liked Peter.

'He is not like the other one. He always greets you and smiles,' the non-whites would say, comparing Peter with Lennie. Like Mr. Bloch he passed jokes now and again when speaking to everybody, black and white.

Even Douglas liked him. He used to say that Peter was easier to get along with because he did not have anything to worry about except passing his examinations and going to open up his own business. He said, 'What's he got to worry about. His father is a Jew who owns a block of flats in the centre of town and has a big business. What else can such a man's son want?'

All this went through my mind as I looked up at Peter crouching next to Douglas and smiling down at Adam. He was holding the screwdriver and swinging it back and forth like a pendulum, without letting it go. Adam raised both his arms, with the palms ready to catch the tool. He was grinning widely. 'So it is talking and playing time,' I thought as I mechanically turned the handle of the addressograph printing machine.

'Catch!' Peter repeated, tugging at Douglas's trousers with his right hand and smiling.

'Look, Dougy, just like my dog. Look at his teeth, just like Dracula!'

Douglas stood still, indifferent. He just kept clicking his tongue. I knew what was on Douglas's mind, he was in one of his moods again. Peter tried to make him smile, tugging at the leg of his trousers again, but without success.

'Ag, that one's a fool!' Douglas said, meaning Adam.

Peter let the screwdriver go and Adam caught it. Peter stood up, looking at Douglas. Then he moved away towards the door. He was running away from Douglas again. I used to feel like running away from him myself when he was in that depressed mood. He used to bring out the bleakest side of our lives as workers, a side I used to try very hard to forget. He said bitterly, 'Adam makes me sick. Him and Lennie are too stupid. They should be working underground in the salt mines, digging salt with shovels!'

'Adam's not a mechanic,' I said. 'Why do you include him?'

'Because he's a fool. I hate him. You know, he could make a lot of dough for himself and yet he sits in one place. Twenty-six years he's worked here, and he still earns seven pounds a week. He's old and finished now. With an empty stomach, he keeps guard over another man's food and doesn't touch it. Why doesn't he pay himself with these goods?'

Peter came up to say, 'I'm going for lunch now, Dougy.'

He smiled at Douglas and patted him on the shoulder. 'Stop moaning, man. I told you before. The boss is too stingy. He just loves money. You can take everything from him – his daughter, even his wife if you like. But you must never touch his money!'

Peter left. Douglas continued complaining. 'I'm getting more sick of this place every day. If Bloch does not give me an "inkrees" this week, you'll see. I'll just stay at home and I won't come to work. The repairs will pile up and he'll be forced to call me back, which thing I'll only do on *my* terms. I did that once four years ago. I just stayed away for three weeks doing odd jobs and repairs for people at home. The boss came to my house personally and begged me to come back to work.'

'And did he give you an increase?' I asked.

'Yes. But that was years ago. My expenses are more now,

my children are growing up and I need more money. You can't stay in one place, can you?'

Douglas went on and on complaining. It became as depressing as it was boring. I felt like running away too, like Adam.

'Peter is not so bad. But that fool, Lennie! You know he has passed matric, can you believe that? And yet he can't even spell "aerial". Have you heard him speak English? It's pathetic, man.'

'But the English-speaking parents complain in the papers that Afrikaans schools get the most First Classes,' I argued.

'They're only fit for the police force, chasing poor natives around day and night for passes,' Douglas said in disgust. 'Most of the time when a job is needed urgently, he calls me to do it. But he earns fifty-six rands and I only earn twenty-four rands, with my fifteen years' experience. I've got a family to support and they are mere boys who have just started working. I can't stand it, I tell you!'

I tried to show him how the boss was not an easy person with money. I could see that, if he could help it, he wouldn't even pay the apprentices what he did pay them. He paid them only because he *had* to. The Wage Board, the Industrial Council and the Trade Union, these all played an important part in protecting the interests and working conditions of the white workers, in determining their salaries, wages, bonuses, medical requirements (not only of the workers, but also those of their dependants and spouses), any various so-called fringe benefits which they enjoyed. Such facilities, I reminded him, were almost non-existent for the non-whites. The non-white workers were unorganised, and it was difficult to get them more organised as the activities of the few trade unions which were trying to function were weakened by the fact that it was illegal for non-whites to strike. What we were paid, therefore, was a matter which rested almost entirely in the hands of the masters. If he 'liked' you and felt that you were a 'good boy or girl', then he paid you a little more than the others.

It was quite evident that Douglas would not be going out for lunch like myself. He complained that he did not have any money to buy lunch, therefore it was pointless to go and sit in the sun. He preferred to talk about our predicament. He remarked that I seemed to be quite satisfied with what I was earning. I hastened to correct this false impression.

'I have often thought of leaving, too, Douglas.'

"Money?"

'No. What's the use of complaining about that? I know I'll get nowhere with that sort of thing. I'm not happy here, Douglas, I'm between two fires. My own people on the one hand, and the white staff on the other. I have a lot of trouble with our African customers. One can understand their attitudes and forgive them. They are suspicious of anyone in a position like mine. They think we are just bent on squeezing money out of them to swell the coffers of our white bosses. The men hate it when I ask to see their passes. They feel that they are being subjected to unnecessary scrutiny, and they can't stand that from a woman! But what I can't stand, is *their* attitude,' I said, indicating the white women seated on the other side. 'With them the thing is a deliberate effort to push me out. They are afraid I am here to compete with them and possibly push *them* out. They can't simply live and let live. If only they could accept that I am just here to do my work and earn my living, all of us would be happier.'

'And the boss, what do you think about him?'

'He's all right, I think. But half the time he does not know what is happening in the office. Not as far as my efficiency is concerned, I mean. He relies almost entirely on the reports he receives from those two, which makes my position quite vulnerable.'

'But he too can be quite nasty sometimes. Like that day when he said that you do not *have* to look at the papers of that customer with the big American car.'

'Which one?' I asked.

'The one who wanted to have a radio fitted into his car. The one with the spotlessly white shirt who had his coat slung over his shoulder and was acting big moving up and down in this passage here brandishing a big bunch of keys trying to impress everybody.'

'Oh, you mean Bembe. I could never forget that name. The one who paid a deposit of one hundred rands. And that was the last time we saw him in this shop! He disappeared without a trace. The boss just could not resist the temptation of accepting that big cash deposit. He just could not bear to give the customer the money back. So he had his car radio installed even though he was quite aware that his particulars were not satisfactory.'

'But why did the boss say that it wasn't necessary for you to see his papers? You always inspect the black customers' documents.'

'The boss told me not to worry because we had taken the registration number of his car, and he had inquired from the garage where the customer had bought the car and been informed that it had been paid for fully in less than six months. That made him a "good" customer, I suppose. I remember the boss saying loudly to his sister after the customer had left: "But

I wonder where he got all that money to pay off such an expensive car within that short time? Maybe he stole it, Lieda?" Mrs. Kuhn answered, "Maybe *they* gave it to him." The boss was still a bit suspicious though; he said, "I do not trust him. How can you trust an informer? Remember what Dad used to say about a spy, Lieda? That an informer is worse than a thief". So Bembe was in fact an informer paid by the police. That was why Mr. Bloch did not want me to see the details in his pass.'

Douglas laughed. We went on talking about the customers and the staff, but all the time I had a notion that he had something on his mind. He spoke of how difficult it was to make money, real money. He said there were ways of making a lot of it without relying on the peanuts which people like him and myself were paid. He said that at times people were not aware of the opportunities they could use.

'For instance, Muriel, in a position such as yours, where you have access to all documents and records, you could make yourself a fortune.'

'How?' I asked, thinking it all sounded too good to be true.

'I know of many Coloured customers who are tired of paying and paying and paying and who would only be happy to have the records of their accounts destroyed. They would give you half the balances of their accounts. All you would need to do would be to pull out the ledger card of that customer and destroy it. Then they would never know how much that customer still owed.'

'They *would* know because we don't just use the ledger cards as a record. There is a register kept of all the accounts and the ledger cards are checked against the register from time to time.'

I lied. In fact no such register was kept at Metropolitan. I just wanted to discourage Douglas from going on with the suggestion. I went on, 'Besides, there are also the invoices we make when the goods are sent out.'

'You could destroy those as well. Just tear them off.'

He was determined to make his case. I was equally determined to make him see the other side.

'I can't do that. The invoices are in numerical order; they follow consecutively. It would therefore be easy to spot a missing number.'

I thought that point would make him change his mind but he came back with, 'Even if they did find that an invoice was missing, they couldn't prove that you did it. It could be any one of the whites, couldn't it? They also steal. Don't you read in the papers about secretaries, managers, and other whites being charged with fraud and other crimes involving money?'

'Yes, but that does not mean that I want to do the same thing. I wouldn't like to appear in court.'

'Oh, you'll never achieve anything sitting there at that lousy desk and being underpaid. Never! You'll sit there holding that pen until you are bent double with age. You must wake up, man.'

'Can't you see that the first person to be suspected would be me because of my colour?' I protested.

'But they would not be *certain*. Haven't you heard how Mrs. Stein was once placed in a responsible position where she dealt with money and she began misappropriating funds? You must have noticed that she very rarely relieves the cashier. They don't trust her near the till. So they could never rule out the possibility that it might have been her.'

Douglas then came up with an alternative suggestion.

'We could get hold of a Coloured customer, or better still, an important-looking Indian one. Suppose he wants to buy an expensive bedroom suite worth about six hundred rands but he's only got two hundred rands. We get him to hand it over to us and pay in sixty or seventy rands as cash deposit. He could produce a false identity card. It could even be one which belonged to a dead man. You know that the boss never looks at the photos. If our customer claimed to be a businessman, say a tailor, the boss would believe him and trust him. He would have a big cash deposit, you see. All you would have to do would be to take down false particulars, that is, false personal references and business references. You know they couldn't get anything from the identity cards Indians and Coloureds carry because they are like those carried by whites.

'Then what?' I asked.

'Then we make sure the customer gives a temporary address. After the goods are delivered the customer removes them. Of course the customer would have to come and pay his instalments regularly for three or four months after the delivery. That would be part of our agreement with the customer. In that way, Mrs. Stein who's so observant, would see the customer always pays at the shop regularly. So when he stops paying, they wouldn't be in any hurry to hunt him out – he having been so important-looking with such a big cash deposit. They would "respect" him and wait for, say, another three months before they started to look for him, by which time of course no one would know anything about such a person. The records would reveal that that particular customer was long dead. Our customer would gain because he would have got an expensive bedroom suite for about a quarter of the price. You and I would have the sixty or seventy rands each. And,' Douglas summed it all up in the broken Afrikaans dialect *tsotsi-taal*, '... *on ons rwa die Jood*' (and we swindle the Jew).

I did not know what to say. I tried to look for any flaws in the scheme, but it all seemed to be a perfect crime which could not fail.

'I could bring a customer this very week,' said Douglas persuasively.

I would have to think of a way out of this, I thought. I would have to procrastinate. I said, 'The best time would be when Mrs. Stein is on holiday. You know she studies the faces of all the customers. She might meet the customer in the street after he had been said to be long dead and send the police to arrest him. If goods were found at his place ...'

Douglas nodded slowly and said, 'You know, I thought you couldn't use your brain, like most women, but now I can see that you can think. I never thought of that. I have worked here for eight years and in all that time I have never known that woman ever going on holiday. If she does go, even if only for a week, we shall all breathe more freely. This shop will be rid of a real menace for that time. I shall hear from you then.'

Douglas was happy, because we had agreed on a deal, a lucrative one. He went over to Gants, bought two cold drinks and offered me one. Although I had agreed, I knew in my heart that I would never be able to go on with it.

That day might have ended as quietly as it had started, if it had not been for one incident which left every member of the staff roaring with laughter, and which remained a joke as long as I was at Metropolitan Radio.

Mr. Bloch and Lennie arrived from town just as I was tidying my desk and everybody was about to go home. Lennie quickly rushed up to the workshop and came down with his coat slung over his arm and carrying a comic in his other hand. He stood looking at the boss who now occupied the chair near the till. Mrs. Kuhn and Mrs. Stein looked at each other. They knew what was coming. Mr. Bloch looked up at the mechanic.

'Yes, Lennie?'

'Mr. Bloch, I would like to sub some money.'

'How much?'

'Ten rands.'

'Ten rands?' Mr. Bloch exclaimed. 'Why so much?'

Everybody was looking at them and listening. Peter and Douglas who were coming down the stairs, also stopped and listened.

'I need it,' Lennie answered.

'What for?' the boss asked frowning.

'I want to go and get married by special licence.'

'*What?* Mr. Bloch exploded into laughter. 'Well, that's the best news I've heard in years!'

By now, almost everyone was laughing, except Mrs. Kuhn who looked more irritated than amused. Mr. Bloch looked back at the mechanic and asked, 'You haven't even got five pounds to pay for a marriage licence but you want to take a wife?'

Douglas was laughing the loudest. He stood near me, looking at the mechanic, who just ignored his stares. Douglas followed me down the passage, saying in Afrikaans, 'Didn't I tell you, Muriel, he's really stupid. He's not marrying for love. All he wants is the money left him by his father. One of the conditions is that he must have attained maturity and be married. He only turned twenty-one last month and the next thing he wants to grab the money. He'll squander it all in no time and then he'll be begging again.'

12
Adam's advice

AFTER BEING absent from work for six days because my child was ill, I experienced a wonderful feeling of satisfaction as I approached the shop. It was like going back where I really belonged.

Adam grinned happily in that friendly way of his, showing nearly all his tobacco-stained teeth, when he saw me pass near the window where he was dusting the articles on display. Inside I could see Ricky, the store-manager, standing speaking to the boss, who was facing away from the door. He looked at me just as I stepped over the threshold. He must have said something to Mr. Bloch because just then the boss quickly turned round and saw me. He waved me back impatiently, the expression on his face like that of a man seeing an apparition.

'Wait, Muriel, don't come in!'

I stood still, confused and perplexed. I did not know what to say. He shouted, 'Why are you here? You ... you're suffering from smallpox, aren't you, or what? Or is it your baby or something? Isn't it?'

I tried to shout back an explanation but he interrupted with something about smallpox, stammering, drowning my voice. Adam stood gaping, his eyes wide open in amazement, looking at the boss and then at me. He asked, 'What's wrong, Muriel, why is the boss so frightened?'

Trying to speak calmly, the boss called to me, 'I think you'd better go home, Muriel. You must understand, I am very sorry, but for the sake of all of us … I – I mean, it's not safe! I need you here, but I think you'd better go.'

Ricky was also trying to say something to the trembling Mr. Bloch, and I waited a little. Mr. Bloch looked at him and suddenly dashed towards the switchboard. I turned towards the door, but the boss shouted at me again, still looking as if I were a leper approaching.

'Wait! Wait, Muriel, I'll ring Doctor Linsk, and find out if it's safe to have you here!'

The boss dialled the number rapidly and nervously. It must have been engaged because he dialled again and again. He put the receiver to his ear and asked me, shouting even louder, 'It's smallpox, isn't it?'

I shouted back, 'No, Mr. Bloch, it's *not* smallpox. It's *chicken-pox,* she's got!'

'What's chicken-pox? Isn't that infectious?'

The boss looked at the store-manager uncertainly while he continued to dial the number.

I stood there motionless and disappointed. I had come back to work so eagerly after spending six days at home. The first three had not been so bad, but as time went on I had become increasingly restless. I had found the days long and had read when I was not attending to the child. But gradually I kept thinking of my work. It was the first week of the month and I knew there would be many customers coming in and many others to pay and make enquiries. It became more and more difficult to concentrate on what I was reading. The location was so desolate during the day, especially when my little Moleboheng was asleep. I had intended to stay with my baby for at least a week, but I felt that my absence from work would inconvenience the office staff which was already short. I could not bear the thought any longer. When the child showed speedy signs of recovery and the dark scabs on her back and chest were falling off, I decided to leave her in the care of a sympathetic friend, and I went back to Metropolitan Radio.

Now I was standing at the door regretting every minute of my impatience and all the hours of unrewarded anxiety. If I had known that Mr. Bloch could manage without me I should have stayed at home. I could have read all the books I had always wished I could find time to read. Imagine. I felt like kicking myself.

Mr. Bloch still could not get through to the doctor. He shouted to me, 'All right, Muriel, don't come in. Just go and do some shopping for about half an hour while I try and get Dr. Linsk on the line, and come back later. The doctor should tell me whether it's safe to have you here or not!'

What a welcome, I thought as I went out. I could not help feeling a little amused. Fancy thinking chicken-pox is small-pox! I remembered how whites always told each other how blacks suffer from all sorts of diseases. That even the slightest physical contact with them can be very dangerous as most of them have unhygienic habits and are carriers of many infectious diseases. But why can they not see that avoiding physical contact will not immunise them? Can't they see that the only way to ensure that the air that *they* breathe and food that *they* eat will not be 'contaminated' by the blacks is by raising their standard of living and giving them adequate education? Surely more and more blacks then would come to appreciate the value of hygiene and clean habits? Surely everyone would gain by that because the two groups can never be separated. Surely it should make the whites concerned that tuberculosis is very rife in the locations, that four out of five Africans suffer from some lung ailment? What is the use of living in fear?

'I hope Mr. Bloch *never* gets through to Dr. Linsk and then I can go back home and do my reading in peace,' I thought crossly.

But I had hardly been five minutes in the supermarket when Johannes rushed in panting breathlessly. From where I was, I could see him looking about and rushing all over the place. His wandering eyes stopped when they spotted me. He came running towards me and gasped, 'Muriel, come quickly. The boss says you must come. Now! He wants you. There are customers waiting.'

I followed Johannes out through the narrow passage. We squeezed our bodies past those of the customers in the queue. The cashier as well as the customers looked at us with expressions of amazement. They must have thought we were a pair of lunatics.

At the door of the store, Adam and the boss were standing and arguing. 'I told you to get more money from that boy who bought the three-band Supersonic Clipper, Adam; what's wrong with you?'

The boss was frowning and asking Adam, who replied, looking at the boss and spreading his arms out, 'He tell me he got no money to eete, Baas. What I can do? Come, Muriel, come!' Adam said, beckoning to me.

I looked at Mr. Bloch. 'All right, Muriel, the doctor says

it's not serious. Sit down there now and attend to that customer. He has thirty rands deposit and wants an Ellis de luxe coal stove.'

It was colder in the shop than outside, but Adam already had the heater on for me. He stood smiling, holding the back of the chair I was about to occupy as if I were the Queen of England. I sat on the chair and thanked Adam. He said, 'I have already cleaned your desk and chair. Just sit down and start. This gentleman is in a hurry.'

And he added under his breath, 'Europeans can be so stupid. They are so afraid of disease. What's the use, they all still die like us, don't they? Just give her your pass book, my brother,' he went on, turning to the customer.

The customer took out the hated document from his back trouser pocket and handed it to me reluctantly. Responding to Adam's remarks, he said, 'And *we* are the ones who do everything for them. Even in their homes *we* cook for them and clean their homes. It is our womenfolk who nurse their babies and give them food.'

We all laughed softly. I took the book and opened it. As I did so, particles of what looked like black dust dropped from it onto the desk. I tried very hard to suppress signs of surprise. I remembered that 'in loyalty to the firm,' customers must be encouraged to buy at all costs. If I showed any signs of disgust, the customer might just decide not to buy after all. Besides, he had not yet given Adam the thirty rands.

As I flapped the hard cover over, I choked. A strong pungent smell emanated from the book, and I started sneezing violently. I went to the kitchen, and drank some water and waited until the sneezing and dizziness had ceased; then I returned, hoping that I would be able to continue.

The customer apologised to me, saying there were perhaps tobacco particles in his passbook. He looked at me and remarked, 'You work nicely here, my sister. Like a white person. You must be very happy to work in such a place.'

'Yes,' I said demurely.

'Look at the heater burning next to you, the telephone and the writing machine ...'

Such remarks were often made by my black customers. I hated them. They gave me that 'white-master's-well-fed-dog' feeling Mangaliso Sobukwe used to tell us about when I was a student at the University of the Witwatersrand. I strove to conceal my true emotions. What could I say?

'The little jobs they did not want to give us at first are being done by us these days,' continued the customer, obviously proud.

I felt like screaming. I was glad when Adam brought the receipt book to the buyer and they left. Adam came and sat on the chair next to me, looking towards the door. He took out a piece of cigarette stump from his shirt pocket, patted his trouser pockets for matches. He put the brown end of the stump between his thick wet lips and kept it there. He looked about and reached for a blank hire purchase agreement form on my desk, and without asking, tore a piece from it.

'What are you doing, Adam! You are wasting it!' I said automatically.

'Ag, never mind. Our baas is too rich. Listen, there is something more important I would like to talk to you about. I want to advise you, Muriel.' He paused, holding the piece of paper he had torn off against the glowing bar of the heater, and when it flamed, he lighted the stump between his lips.

'You see, my child, I know you have gone to school and

learnt much and perhaps you think you know more than I do about life generally ...'

Just then Mrs. Kuhn's voice called sharply from the other side, 'Adam, come here, quick!' When Adam was near her, the boss's sister ordered, 'Give me that typewriter there. No, not that, the typewriter on Mrs. Stein's desk, man! Oh, Adam, you're really getting old. Look at him, Mrs. Stein, he's giving me the adding machine instead of the typewriter!'

Mrs. Stein only nodded her head and went on adding loudly, '... *vyf, elf, agtien – Een honderd, agt-en-twintig Rand, tien sent.'* * She always added figures in Afrikaans. Then she said, 'Yes, Mrs. Kuhn, he's getting older and more stupid by the day. Have you noticed how he dusts the furniture? He can't stand on his feet any more. He leans on it with one elbow, and wipes with the other arm, while all the ash from the cigarettes he always has between his lips drops on the furniture.'

'It's his bunions, Mrs. Stein,' Mrs. Kuhn replied. 'Hey, Adam, what happened to those bunions, those corns, Adam, are they finished now?'

Adam ignored them completely. They might just as well have been speaking to a wall. He moved away from them, and came slouching towards me. He looked annoyed. Mrs. Kuhn asked him again, 'Adam, why don't you answer?' She and Mrs. Stein laughed.

'Why don't you say something, Adam?' I asked him, and he replied in vernacular, 'Do you answer a lunatic's questions? It's only because the baas is not here. As soon as the baas goes, they start their nonsense. Now, you listen to me, Muriel. You have acquired much of the knowledge of the white man's life, but I

---

* 'Five, eleven, eighteen – One hundred and twenty-eight Rand, ten cents.'

can see that you are in fact ignorant. Some things in life the white man knows nothing about. You are weak, my child. You must ask your husband to speak to his parents to get you a good African witch-doctor to strengthen you against some of these evil spirits. If you are weak, these things can be dangerous.'

He paused for a while. He was stern and spoke with the typical authority of a man of his age.

'Look how you behaved this morning when that customer came to you with that pass which had been "worked on". You must be very careful. It can happen that a man whose aim may be to "get" you, can come here and cast a spell over you so powerful that you can actually leave your house and your husband and children and go running after him!'

I laughed, but Adam was in earnest. He went on seriously. 'For instance, consider this illness of your child which kept you away from work for so long. That should *not* have happened. If you had taken your child to *our* doctors it would have been better. It would have saved you a lot which you suffered this morning when you tried to enter through that door. You must get someone to work on you. Do you remember how I used to be in pain, how my arm used to be sore from the neck right down to my fingers and how it used to hang sluggishly and useless so that I could not even move the furniture? Do you remember how even the boss used to call a white doctor to examine me in the shop here and how many times that doctor came to give me injections? Did all that help? Never. Finally I decided to go and see one of our own witch-doctors, and here I am today all fit and strong ...'

Mrs. Kuhn's voice, shrill and loud, interrupted our talk.

'I keep on striking the wrong keys. I just can't concentrate with Adam's voice over there. Muriel, Adam's talking too much. Just chase him away!'

'He was telling me about his arm, Mrs. Kuhn,' I explained.

'But his arm's better. He doesn't complain about the pains any more.'

'He says it's because he went to a witch-doctor, Mrs. Kuhn, when the white doctors couldn't cure him. He said I should go there too and take my baby.'

'Oh, Adam talks a lot of nonsense,' said Mrs. Kuhn.

He went over to the other side and pulled his khaki coat-sleeve right up to show the line of black marks and incisions left by the witch-doctor's sharp blade.

'Look, missus, look,' he said going nearer.

'Oh Adam, go away! Why can't you tell your girl-friend or wife to wash your coat and iron it? It looks terrible.'

Adam's face assumed that hard impenetrable mask of in-difference once again. He adjusted his coat sleeve and walked away.

I looked at Adam as he moved away, thankful that he was going towards the linoleum, and not coming to compel me to answer the questions he had asked me as I might have disap-pointed him. He had imparted part of his extensive knowledge to me, a lot of which still remains inside that head of his. He slowly slouched back to his post, the soles of his unlaced worn shoes hardly leaving the surface of the floor, but rubbing over it with every step. He gave me one more knowing look and shook his head slowly, perhaps regretting my apparent state of utter ignorance and stubbornness. He sat, sullen, facing the door, his eyes staring, his lips partially parted. He sat dead still, big and rugged like the sphinx, as if he was part of the furni-ture, stiff and static.

13

Friday

It was Friday. For most workers this meant pay day. The blacks poured into the towns in hundreds of thousands. The labourers, factory-workers, garage-workers, office-workers; and so-called shop-girls and shop-boys, tea-boys and tea-girls, flat-girls and flat-boys – in fact, so-called 'boys' and so-called 'girls' of every age and description – all were hurrying towards their places of employment where their white masters and white mistresses were waiting for them.

One could never mistake this day for any other. Even if I had been unconscious for weeks and recovered consciousness on this day, I would be able to tell without the slightest hesitation that it was Friday. Just by looking around and observing the movements of the people, their gait and gestures; by the tones of their high-pitched voices, I would know. The atmosphere was loaded with expectation.

The pay packet is a strange force. Just the prospect alone of receiving it – irrespective of its size and the value of its contents – has an intoxicating effect.

At Metropolitan Radio on this particular Friday Johannes was already sweeping the front pavement of the shop when I arrived. He was humming a tune, the dirty duster hanging out of the pocket of his khaki overall flapped as he worked with a marked spring in his step. He smiled broadly as I approached him.

'Good morning, Johannes,' I said. 'Has Adam arrived already?'

'Yes, he has just come. I have been here nearly an hour already and I live far away, near Vereeniging. You and Adam live only about sixteen miles out of Jo'burg but ...'

'But I have a lot to do at home before I come to work.'

A European man followed close behind me as I walked up the passage. He had a pink face and an untidy mop of very white hair. He walked with a stoop and a slight limp. He must be a beggar, I thought.

I greeted Mr. Bloch who was standing on the other side of the counter as I passed to my desk. Looking at the man behind me, he asked impatiently, 'What do you want?'

'I just want some money to buy some food.'

'To eat or to drink?' the boss asked him.

'To eat of course,' the man replied, looking at Mr. Bloch and trying very hard to look convincing.

'Not to go and buy a bottle of beer at the bar?'

'No.'

'All right, wait here,' Mr. Bloch said, putting his hand into his trouser pocket and taking out a twenty-cent piece. He called Adam. 'Adam, go and buy a loaf of bread and a pint of milk.'

Mrs. Kuhn looked scornfully at the beggar and remarked, 'He is disappointed. He thought you were going to give him the money so that he could go straight to the bar.'

'Where is Mrs. Stein, Lieda?' asked Mr. Bloch. 'Hasn't she arrived yet?'

'No. She'll perhaps be late. She wasn't well yesterday,' his sister replied.

At nine o'clock Lambert, as usual, brought the time sheets for the store. He put these on the desk usually occupied by Mrs. Stein. He looked around an asked me softly: 'Where's Mrs. Stein? She had better hurry up. We want our pay early today.'

'Larry, if Mrs. Stein doesn't come in today who'll do the wages?' asked Mrs. Kuhn.

Mr. Bloch shrugged his shoulders. 'You'll have to do it, Lieda. Who else do you think can?'

Mrs. Kuhn looked at me. 'You see, Muriel? Never work for relations. They always expect too much from you. He doesn't think I get tired!'

The so-called lorry-boys and their so-called boss-boy, Agrippa, greeted me loudly in high spirits not shared by the office staff. To them, it meant there would be more work, possibly no lunch-hour, nervous strain, trying to find record cards for customers who wanted to know what their balances were. And this was no ordinary Friday. It was also the end of the month. Mrs. Stein had worked very hard this week and the previous week sending out thousands of letters. The last batch of statements and invoices had also been posted a week ago. More outgoing letters and statements brought more money, more phone calls and queries, enquiries and complaints, and also to some customers, more disillusionment and disappointments.

Lennie's footsteps distracted our attention. He was stamping heavily on the plank floor of the 'attic' less than three feet above our heads with feet like those of a stampeding cow.

'Lennie, man, please, man, walk like a person not like a horse, for goodness sake, man,' shouted the boss.

Lennie laughed. He also seemed excited with the payday elation. He descended the stairs and asked Adam, 'What's wrong, Adam?'

'Baas Lennie, dis custom is kros. She say portabol still no gudu and she pay ten rands las week when you finish repair.'

The customer did look cross. I could see her speaking and gesticulating, looking from Adam to Lennie, explaining what was wrong with her radio. She addressed Adam harshly but spoke politely to the white mechanic. Poor Adam, as usual, was paying the price of being black.

Lennie called me over to help. They were standing round a portable radio, a four-band Omega which stood neatly on the desk on several layers of cloth in which it had been wrapped, like a beloved infant who was again brought to the doctor for medical examination, and whose mother was standing by, worried by its painful relapse.

Lennie looked bored and impatient. He was turning the knobs and pressing the buttons on the radio. I listened to what the customer had to say. She could speak English quite fluently and I wondered why the mechanic had asked for my assistance.

'Master, listen. This radio doesn't speak Zulu after five o'clock.'

Lennie replied impatiently, 'But *there's* Zulu.' He said, turning to me, 'Muriel, please explain to her. Maybe it was the battery, it was weak. There. I've put in a new battery and it sounds different already.'

I repeated what the mechanic said, and interpreted her reply. 'She's not concerned about the tone. She says after five o'clock every evening, the radio just stops playing.'

'What's wrong, is it bewitched?' Adam asked the customer in vernacular. The customer looked at him and said, 'Yes, you bewitched it here. You want me to come and pay more money. You only half fix it up.'

'Where do you living, far?' Lennie asked, thinking that perhaps if she lived too far from the nearest F.M. tower the distance might affect its reception. Instead of addressing the mechanic, she turned to Adam and myself, and spoke sharply, pointing and almost shouting, *'Mona, Berario mona. Qholong ea nta mona!'* (Here, in Berrario, just here. On the hip-joint of a louse!)

'Well,' Lennie said, turning to Adam, 'I can't go with her to Berrario to test it and see whether she is speaking the truth or not. It shouldn't make any difference to the reception if she lives in Berrario.'

Whereupon, the mechanic went back to the workshop, stamping and whistling. Adam went on trying to convince her that there was nothing wrong with the portable. Mr. Bloch was busy on the telephone and he did not want to disturb him.

Adam said, 'Look, my sister, speak the truth and shame the devil. Your battery was an old one. We have given you a new battery and the thing already plays better. You can have the battery for nothing. Go now, please.'

The customer wrapped the radio carefully in the cloths and left the shop, still cursing and threatening Adam. He was listening to the boss struggling on the phone.

'What, what are you saying, what is your name?' Then looking at me, 'Oh, Muriel, please just take this call on your desk there. It will take hours trying to get her name alone. It sounds like "gogga" to me.'

And he grumbled to his sister, 'I'm telling you – these people should not speak on the phone, man. You ask for her name, she gives you a number like she is a convict. You see. They do not think like us.'

After I had taken down the message he asked me, 'What does she want, what is her name, Muriel?'

'Her name is Legina Rorwana, Mr. Bloch,' I said.

'Now why did she say "gogga"? I'm sure she said "gogga" to me.'

'No, Mr. Bloch, the R is pronounced like G in Afrikaans. Like the R in Radebe,' I tried to explain to him.

'She wants us to send an agent to collect twenty rands, the balance on the portable. She is leaving for the Transkei.'

'So if we hadn't found out what she wanted, she'd have left for the Transkei with the twenty rands *and* the portable! Honestly, these people!'

I went back to my desk thinking about the customer with the portable radio. Some Africans, I knew, believed that the dealers from whom they bought their radios had the power to make their sets play or stop no matter how far away the dealer may be from the radio. In fact, quite a number of African customers would come in to pay their instalments, and would then ask the boss to 'make' their sets play as they had paid up their arrears.

Mr. Bloch took advantage of these beliefs, and on several occasions, I would hear him threaten a 'slow' customer with: 'If you do not pay properly, your radio will get cross and stop playing.'

Mr. Bloch soon called me to attend to another black customer.

'Muriel, just explain to this customer about the hire purchase price.'

'Why does he want to run away when I bought the stove from him?' the woman asked in vernacular.

'He's not running away,' I explained. 'He's busy, and he

wants me to explain to you, maybe he can't speak so that you understand.' But she followed the boss who had gone to serve some white customers and asked him, 'Master, why is your increase so much?'

'Oh, for goodness sake, man, I told you, it's not "increase", it's interest.' He looked impatient but he went on, 'Look, if I borrow money from the bank, I can't expect them to lend it for nothing, can I?'

The boss moved away. The woman stood looking at me in bewilderment.

I tried to explain. 'You see, instead of having to pay cash for the stove, they let you have it now and then for helping you like that, you have to pay a little more money on top.'

'You say little but it's so much. Eighty pounds. When shall I finish it? I haven't even got a husband and they've already taken my old stove away!'

She looked as if she was going to start crying any moment. I tried to show her that it wasn't as bad as it seemed.

'Just go on paying a little bit every month. Three pounds, three pounds every month … In two years you'll have paid for it.'

She looked at me as if I were a traitor, and went away without saying goodbye.

It was now quite evident that Mrs. Stein was not coming to work. We were now very busy. As soon as I had finished dealing with one customer, Mr. Bloch would have another one waiting for me. He handed me a letter, what we called the 'green letter', claiming from Albanus Ntshingila immediate payment of all the arrears – which amounted to R236.70 – and threatening court action.

Albanus Ntshingila denied any knowledge of such arrears.

He claimed that his son had been paying the account regularly, and that only a few rands were still outstanding on the radiogram and studio couch.

'All right, Albanus,' said Mr. Bloch, 'you say you have been paying regularly every month. The Credit Department says that you have that big balance still outstanding. Our records cannot be wrong. All the balances are done by machine. Where are your receipts to show that you have been paying?'

The customer replied, 'They are with my son. He has been paying every month.'

'Did your son ever show you the receipts?'

'Do you think my son is a liar?'

'All right then, Albanus, you wait here while Muriel finds your card and then we shall see.'

When I could not find the card among the 'Ntsh-' lot I went right through the Ns – and there were approximately one hundred of them – but without success. I asked the customer to show me his pass book so that I might check the spelling but the name in the pass book and in the letter were the same. Then I went through the Ts, just in case the initial letter had been left off, as sometimes happened. Mrs. Kuhn spared a few minutes from the wages book to look through the Ns in the Europeans' ledger cards in case it had been filed in that tray by mistake.

'Mrs. Stein must have hidden it on purpose,' Mrs. Kuhn remarked sharply to me. 'She's underhand, that woman. For instance, she smokes and hides that she does. What does she think we are, small kids? Everytime she goes to the toilet she takes her handbag. Why do you think she does that? It just goes to show you what kind of a person she is. Everything must be underhand.'

All the white staff were now less cautious, less guarded when they spoke to me. She went back to the wage calculations, forgetting that she had boasted that morning that she would finish in half the time it took Mrs. Stein.

Mr. Bloch had already asked me twice if I could not find the card. I began to panic. Oh God, please let me find it, I prayed. I must find it. If I failed to find it, it would not be because it was misfiled. It would be because I was black – and black is synonymous with stupid.

Then suddenly I had a brainwave. (Who said prayers are never answered!) I asked the customer, 'Haven't you got another name, your father's perhaps, or something?'

'Oh well, my father's name was Kubheka. But we hardly ever use that one,' he replied.

I immediately looked under the Ks, and there I found the card. Next to 'Albanus Ntshingila', the name 'Kubheka' was added in pencil.

Albanus now revealed that while he was ill in hospital, his son had pledged that he would pay for the goods. As the surname on Albanus's son's pass-book was Kubheka, Mrs. Stein had apparently added it in pencil and filed it under K and not N.

I was exhausted. I felt as if I had run a marathon race. But we hadn't finished yet.

'Tell him, Muriel,' Mr. Bloch was saying. 'Tell him his good son only *promised* to pay six months ago. That was the last we saw of him. And tell him that *he* signed the H.P. so I expect *him* to pay, not his son, or uncle, or mother or wife or anything like that. I've got nothing to do with any of them and I don't want a lot of talk, talk, talk. I want my money, that's all. Tell him!'

I told the customer what the boss had said. He was abject.

'Tell the boss that I'm very sorry, and please he must give

me a chance. I'll come in tomorrow – Saturday, without fail.'

Mr. Bloch nodded and said, 'All right, that's enough now, Muriel, other customers are waiting. Put the card back now, and make a note "Customer promised to come and pay Saturday. If no payment, repossess goods".'

'Agrippa!' Mrs. Kuhn called out. 'Where is he? For the last three hours, him and his boys have been moving in and out of the kitchen, looking at me with hungry eyes as they pass. What do they think I am, a speeding machine or something?'

Mr. Bloch replied, 'I've sent him out, Lieda. Why do you want him?'

'I wanted to find out from him if any of his boys had been absent. They couldn't all have worked the whole week, they never do.'

'He'll come back at two, Lieda. I have instructed him to go and load off the repossessed goods at the store-room and to go and collect goods for delivery from the shops in town and be back at two.'

The telephone rang. It was the other branch in town. Mr. Bloch shouted into the mouthpiece, 'Who it is, a *soggen*? Oh well, with a *soggen* you can go as high as you want to. Up to 37 per cent you can charge. Which bedroom suite do they want, that Marquise with the triple rectangular mirrors on the dressing-table? Will they be able to pay the instalment?' He switched from English to Yiddish.

Johannes was standing at the entrance to the kitchen, listening. He liked interpreting to me what was said in Yiddish. He came over to me and whispered, 'The boss says "where do they get all that money from when they are kaffirs" – that's what that word *soggen* means – a black person like you and me.'

He moved away, his eyes fixed on the wages book which

Mrs. Kuhn had in front of her. She looked at him absent-mindedly. She must have been thinking of her Saturday off, because she grumbled to herself, 'If he wants me to come tomorrow, I'm finished. I wonder why she chose not to come to work on a Friday – wanted a long weekend, I suppose.'

She noticed Johannes staring at her and spoke sharply.

'No use looking at me like that. You have no money today. Why did you sub so much money?'

'What can I do, missus? I got children.'

Mrs. Kuhn went on grumbling to herself. 'Staying away on Friday like this! There was nothing wrong with her, nothing. I can't stand that woman. Now I've got to do the wages. What about all those agreements waiting to be typed? And it's the end of the month! I must do the books, cheques must be made out. She doesn't care, I tell you she doesn't!'

There was not going to be a Saturday off for her that week, and she was bitter.

More customers came in to pay and waited in a queue impatiently twisting bank-notes in their hands. Johannes looked at the customers and then at me and shook his head. 'My God, this man makes money. If I were him, with so much money coming to me every day, I would eat so much that I wouldn't be able to breathe when I go to bed at night!'

Adam walked into the shop followed by a Coloured woman and her daughter. He called, 'Muriel, come and help me with these customers, please.'

They wanted to buy a kitchen table, four chairs and a perambulator for the woman's grandchild. When I gave Mr. Bloch the completed hire purchase forms, he looked at the name and asked, 'Why is the name on the identity card different?'

'Mrs. Singh was formerly Mrs. Davids. She was recently

married to Mr. Singh, and the name on her identity card has not yet been changed. She showed me her marriage certificate, Mr. Bloch.'

Mr. Bloch took my word for it. 'Oh, the lady was Mrs. Davids, and now she "singhs".' He laughed, but the customer did not. She asked, 'When will you deliver the pram? My daughter here is in rather a hurry for that. The table and chairs I am not so worried about.'

'Well, if you are in such a hurry, I don't mind. You can put your daughter in the pram and push it home to Albertsville!' Mr. Bloch was irrepressible.

It was now about 12.45 p.m. and the boss was about to go for lunch. It was the only leisure he allowed himself – an hour to an hour-and-a-half on Fridays sitting down for refreshments while discussing recent developments and trends in the business world with a friend.

He handed the H.P. agreement to the cashier at the till. 'Make out a receipt for this twenty rand to this customer. And please give me five rands there for my lunch, I'll sign for it.'

Then turning to his sister, he said, 'Lieda, just keep an eye here, I'm going for lunch with the bank manager.'

Mrs. Kuhn called out, 'Adam, where are you? Where is he? He's gone again. He's never there when you want him!'

'Yes, missus,' Adam answered from the door.

'Just watch the door. Nothing must walk out, eh?'

'Yes, missus.'

Mrs. Kuhn put on her reading glasses and went on with the calculation of the wages, moaning softly to herself. 'How does he expect me to do the wages, make out the cheques and watch the staff at the same time? I can't take this. He must get more staff. Reliable staff, that's all.'

Adam got up from the boss's chair, where he was dreamily sitting and staring, and went towards the kitchen and the 'Whites Only' lavatory that I had been forbidden to use.

A white customer walked in and asked for a small portable radio. Mrs. Kuhn stood up, went to the shelves and produced one in a leather case.

'What's the price?' the customer asked.

'Adam!' called Mrs. Kuhn. 'Where is he?'

'Yes, missus!' Adam answered from the lavatory.

'Come here!' Mrs. Kuhn did not want to keep the customer waiting.

'Weite bite, missus, I coming!' Adam shouted back. But I could hear that he was still busy.

After he had finished, he hurriedly came back, not bothering to wash his hands. He gave the price of the radio, but the customer only nodded and left.

I asked him in vernacular, 'Adam, why did you go into that toilet without bothering even to shut the door?'

'I have to hurry back and watch the door, don't I? If anything gets stolen, I'm always to blame. They take it out of my pay.'

'But why did you not shut the door, Adam? The ladies ... everybody could hear.'

He answered unconcerned, 'What ladies? I do not care about them. This is not their shop. It's Mr. Bloch's shop. Do you think I am as scared of them as you are?' And he added bitterly, 'I am not supposed to go out, so I use their toilet and I don't care!'

It was no use trying to speak to him. The long, painful years of contact with the whites had developed within him a hard protective core of indifference to all their constant abusive reprimands. He was dead inside, I thought.

After 2 p.m. the boss walked in. His eyes were bloodshot and his breathing was audible. The air, passing through his hairy nostrils, produced a hissing sound, like a breeze passing over reeds. I could hear that as he passed behind me, removing his jacket and hanging it on the 'Whites Only' rack.

'Hoza,* Satan!' he shouted. 'Where is he, where's Agrippa?'

It was still Friday. Time for business. No dragging of feet now, work, work. Agrippa emerged from the kitchen.

'Come on, man, get a "moowe" on now, man. Go and deliver the goods.' Then turning to me the boss asked, 'Where are those deliveries I asked you to make out this morning, Muriel? Did you give them to me?'

'Yes, Mr. Bloch.'

Taking the delivery notes from his drawer, he went out followed by Agrippa. Mrs. Kuhn had at last finished calculating the wages. She sent Adam to the bank for cash, and crouched over the journal, making entries.

A white customer came in to collect his portable radio which he had brought in for repair a week ago. It was not ready. Lennie had been working on it. The boss went up to the workshop with the customer, saying 'Let's go and see what's happening up there.'

'I can't stand that thing, you know,' burst out Mrs. Kuhn, looking at me.

'Which thing, Mrs. Kuhn?'

'Lennie!' she snarled.

The two of them had not been on speaking terms since they quarrelled over his leave pay and bonus about a year ago.

Adam came back from the bank and put the money-bags

---

* Come. (Nguni)

with the money for the wages on the desk in front of Mrs. Kuhn who began to count it and put it into the envelopes.

A traveller walked in and stood at the counter, facing Mr. Bloch. He came from Pretoria, he said, and he wanted to sell the boss linoleum squares.

'You want me to buy lino squares; what will I do with them?' asked Mr. Bloch.

'Sell them,' the traveller replied.

'Who'll buy them?' Mr. Bloch asked, looking at the customers as they came to pay. 'Even a *soggen* doesn't want to buy ordinary lino. They prefer rubber lino, because it's stronger. Besides, I only make one rand profit on a lino square. Everyone who buys one wants it delivered. By the time I've paid my boys for loading it on and loading it off, including the transportation costs, I've already lost on it. It's not a good proposition.'

'My sister, what's the price of the small radios in the window?' A customer was calling me.

'What's he saying, Muriel?' Mr. Bloch scented business.

'He wants to know how much the small portable radios are, Mr. Bloch,' I said.

'Six pounds, nineteen and six. Does he want one?'

The customer asked, 'Does it catch everything?'

'Yes, you catch everything there, English station, Afrikaans station, even Police station you catch,' Mr. Bloch said, smiling at the customer, who laughed.

'Is it F.M.?' he asked.

'No, it's not F.M. You want F.M.?' He called out, 'Adam, where are you? Come and show him a small F.M. portable. A one-band Tempest maybe.'

He went back to his chair to drink his tea and chat with the traveller whose linoleum he would not buy.

In the kitchen, Johannes was complaining bitterly. 'You know, these people beat me. Fancy not recognising me.'

'Who?'

'The whites.'

'Why, Johannes?'

'I've been working for his brother for twelve years and he can't even recognise me. I passed right in front of him and even looked into his face with the hope that he might say Hello, but he didn't even know me.' He shook his head. He was taking it so seriously that I could not help laughing.

'Maybe he did recognise you but he just did not say Hello.'

'After twelve years?' he asked emphatically.

Hearing Johannes complain, Adam asked the traveller whether he recognised Johannes. Just then Mr. Bloch and the traveller laughed.

'Listen,' I said to Johannes.

Mr. Bloch was asking the traveller, 'Why did he leave?'

'He wanted more money, and they wouldn't pay him.'

'So he did recognise me after all,' Johannes was pleased. Adam came into the kitchen. I asked him, 'Did *you* ask the traveller whether he recognised Johannes, Adam?'

'Yes. I'm not scared to ask him. That boy, he was only a child when I started working for Mr. Bloch,' Adam said loudly. I was thankful that he was speaking in vernacular.

'Are they relations?'

'Yes, most of these Johannesburg Jews are related to each other. Even if they are not, they know each other.'

Adam left the kitchen and I followed. The traveller had gone. Mr. Bloch stood looking at the long queue of customers with pleasure.

'What's that one waiting for, Adam? He has been there half-an-hour already.'

'He want outside serviss for radio, baas.'

'What's your name?' Mr. Bloch asked the customer.

'Elias.'

'What's wrong with Elias's radio, Adam?' the boss asked taking the service book from the counter, and bringing it to me.

'He gote no vois, baas.' Some of the customers started giggling.

'Muriel, just make out a service card to Elias – Pilot Belafonte radiogram – To check volume control and all transmissions. And just mark it "Urgent" in block letters, eh?'

I did as he instructed. Elias was still standing. Mr. Bloch looked at him and said, 'All right now, Elias. I'll bring him in, the radio.'

He signalled for the customer to go but the customer was reluctant. The boss repeated, 'All right, you can go now. I'll fetch him.'

The boss was in the habit of deliberately speaking broken English when addressing African customers as you do when you speak to a child. The customer was still not satisfied. He had been coming to complain about his radiogram so many times, and was now obviously sceptical and suspicious of the boss's ability to keep a promise.

'Adam, tell him, I'll send Henry tonight to collect it. All right, take this, here …' The boss pushed his thumb and forefinger into his trouser pocket and handed a five cent coin to the customer. 'Take this, and go and buy yourself a cold drink.'

Elias took the coin, smiling, and walked away towards the door.

One of the customers waiting for her radio, said to me in

vernacular, 'You work for a very good boss, eh?'

But I was thinking of times when the boss's mood was not so well disposed towards impatient customers. I remembered one busy day when the boss was speaking to an elderly white couple, and Doris, a 'good' customer, came to enquire about her radiogram, which had been out of order for some time. She had received no response to her request for a mechanic to repair it, and so she was annoyed with the management, which she claimed had treated her badly. She started 'performing', as they say.

'*Hei, tula wena,* shut up, don't come and make a noise here!' the boss shouted at her from where he was sitting with the couple.

Doris was adamant and furious. She wasn't going to be frightened into obedience so easily when she had been paying her money regularly. She had shouted back, 'You can go and fetch that rubbish back, if you can't repair it!'

'Shut up, you don't own this shop! This is not Zambia!'

I learned later that the white couple were from Zambia. They had come back to dear old South Africa to settle permanently, saying that the Africans in Zambia treated the whites there with contempt.

But today Mr. Bloch was in affable mood. A very tall African customer came in to pay. Mr. Bloch looked at him, smiling, and greeted him with: '*Molo, Fitshan*' (short one), you come pay?'

'Yes, I've come to pay but I'm not short. You are short and you call me "short one".'

Mr. Bloch laughed, grabbing the receipt book the customer was holding out.

'Now what's your name?' he asked. 'Daniel? Daniel who, Daniel Satan?'

'Sethabela, not Satan,' the customer repeated, offended now.

'Oh, *haikona** Satan?' Everybody laughed.

I felt like a breath of fresh air. A few minutes outside in the yard would not matter, I thought, and went out.

I would have enjoyed the cool breeze and the sunshine if it had not been for the Portuguese, or Greek, or Italian, kids whose families occupied the cheap flats above the shop next door. They were, as usual, badly behaved and they kept throwing stones at me and laughing. To them all people with black faces were objects you may amuse yourself with.

Ben, the yard and flat cleaner, came along singing loudly. I could see that he had already gulped a few cartons of *Ndambula.*† He was happy. It was Friday afternoon, and of course he had made quite a lot of extra money from letting his room. He came to my rescue at once.

'*Hei, voetsek* you!'‡ he shouted, picking up stones to throw at the kids, who scattered, laughing and running in all directions. They stood a safe distance away, laughing and jeering, sticking their pink tongues out and making eyes at us.

'Thank you, Ben, but don't throw stones at those kids. One of these days you'll lose your job and that valuable room of yours,' I said.

'Why should I?' he asked, looking at me.

'Their fathers will either kill you or throw you into the street.'

'Not when some of their fathers are my best customers.

---

*   no.

†   a home brew, usually highly intoxicating.

‡   You go away! From *hei*, you (when pointing at the person or animal that you are addressing), and *voetsek*, a short form of *voet sê ek*: go, I say (usually used in driving away a dog). (Afrikaans)

They are my brothers-in-law at night when the lights are out.'

I went out of the yard into the street. Outside on the pavements, there were hundreds of people (mostly blacks) milling along the narrow pavements, hurrying to catch their homeward-bound trains.

These fast-moving multitudes are the black proletariat. The sunny Republic of South Africa – the white man's paradise – would never tick without them. To their labour the Republic owes her phenomenal industrial development. If they were suddenly to divert their course of movement now, at this moment, to their so-called homelands instead of to the locations on fringes of the 'white' towns, the white masters would go down on their knees to beg them to remain. As I slowly made my way back to the shop, I thought, our leaders, most of them in exile, others buried alive, and others already dead, were right – a sit-down strike throughout the country lasting only two weeks would bring the whole paradise crumbling down!

At the till, writing out receipts, was the boss himself.

'What's your name?'

'Johanna Mngqxengeza,' the customer replied.

'What? Just spell your second name.'

The customer faltered, uncertain. I spelt it for the boss who remarked, shaking his head, 'No wonder we can't find the cards the way they spell their names. How am I to know when the owner of the name doesn't know herself?'

Johannes was standing on the other side of the steel railings without his khaki overall. In one hand, he was holding his *kirrie** with his hat propped over the knob. It was nearly time for him to go home. He left an hour earlier on week-days, as he

---

*   walking stick. (Afrikaans)

133

lived so far away from Johannesburg. He was moaning and grumbling.

'*Tlisa chelete, Morena.*' (Bring the money, my Lord), Johannes said, his palm open, ready to receive. The boss guessed what he wanted. He asked him, 'What money, Johannes? There's no money for you. You subbed all your money during the week.'

'Ag, baas!' Johannes said, withdrawing his hand slowly but keeping his eyes fixed on the boss.

'Shop!' Adam shouted from the other end of the shop, near the entrance. He meant that a white customer had come in. The boss immediately moved out of the 'office' to the customer, ignoring Johannes, who also went towards the entrance, throwing his hands about, wielding the *kirrie* in disgust.

'They don't care ... I shall never catch the train ... they can keep their money ...'

For him, Friday had not ended as happily as he had expected. He had gone home disappointed, without his pay packet.

At five o'clock Agrippa was lingering hopefully. The boss said, pointing at Agrippa, 'Lieda, just let me pay them. This baboon will never go without his pay.'

His sister handed him the pay envelopes. Agrippa, smiling, called in his 'boys'. The other workers from the storeroom also came in and stood in a group, facing the boss. Mr. Bloch put the envelopes on the desk in front of him. Then his attention was attracted by a white couple who were walking in. The 'boys' and the customers stood aside to let them pass. European customers never stood in a queue. As a rule, they were served immediately they entered the shop and not with other, black, customers.

'Can I help you?' the boss asked the well-dressed white man.

'Yes. I want to buy a portable radio for a child. She'll be six on Sunday.'

The boss put the pay envelopes inside the till and went to the showcase from where he brought a small two-band portable in a leather case. He switched it on and it started playing.

'This should do for a child of six. It's got a medium waveband and one short waveband,' he said, showing it to the couple.

'Hasn't it got F.M.?' asked the man, frowning.

'I can give you one, but the price is more than double, just because of the F.M. It's really not worth it, for a child,' the boss said.

'It's meant for a birthday present. I think this one will do, darling,' the woman said to her husband.

'Yes. You don't actually need F.M. F.M. is for *Muntus*,'* the boss said, smiling and looking provokingly at Lambert, who was standing with the other 'boys' from the store.

'Yes,' Lambert replied. 'The *Muntus* must pay heavily for their indoctrination.'

After the customer had paid for the radio and left, the boss turned to his sister and asked, 'Why is Lambert and the others here, Lieda, didn't you send their pay down to the store?'

'Who would I send? Lennie's alone upstairs,' his sister replied.

'He's a politician. Give him his pay and let him go.'

'You've got all the envelopes, Larry.'

The boss opened the till and took out the envelopes. He handed Lambert his first, saying, 'When are you going to shave off that terrible beard of yours, can't you afford a razor blade?'

---

* plural of *Muntu*, a person or human being. (Nguni)

Lambert replied, 'I'll shave it off the day our leaders come back from Robben Island!'

Agrippa and his 'boys' were waiting. They marched slowly along the narrow passage, in a long single-file procession towards the counter, their faces solemn, like communicants. The long-awaited moment had at last arrived – they were going to receive remuneration for their labour.

The boss handed them their pay envelopes one by one.

'There you are, Chimp,' he said to John Msiza.

Msiza was nicknamed John the Chimp by the white staff because of his extraordinarily thick lips, and to differentiate him from Long John, the tall hefty Zulu, who never smiled.

John Msiza took his pay from the boss with both hands cupped.

'There you are, Long John.' The tall one took it with neither smile nor thanks.

'There, Madala,' the boss said to Aaron, who looked old because of his bald head.

Agrippa was looking on, amused, like a captain, proud to present his crew to a high-ranking admiral.

'There you are, Makuluskop,' he said to Daniel. I could never guess why he had nicknamed him 'Big Head' because his head looked normal to me.

It was now Agrippa's turn. Mrs. Kuhn looked up at the tall Swazi lorry-driver and shook her head.

'*He* would never go without his pay! And now he's going straight to the nearest shebeen with the load of goods. The deliveries will only be done tonight in the dark, and the customers will be coming to complain tomorrow again.'

'Go now, go, Agrippa,' said Mr. Bloch, 'and don't let those boys of yours scratch the goods, eh? Don't take those goods to the shebeen, deliver them to the customers.'

Agrippa just smiled in reply. Taking the envelope the boss had given him, he looked at it carefully and put it in his shirt pocket. Ignoring Mrs. Kuhn, he said to me, 'Good night, my sister.'

'Good night, Agrippa.'

It was Friday evening. The speeding multitudes had thinned down. Most had gone home, taking with them the precious pay envelopes.

It was time for the office staff to go home too. I had finished clearing my desk and I took up my handbag.

'Good night, Mr. Bloch,' I said to the boss.

But half-way down the passage I met a customer who had dashed in hurriedly. He was carrying an old portable radio in one hand and a pay envelope in the other. Mr. Bloch called, 'Just come back, Muriel, please!'

At the counter he said, reaching for the service book and handing it to me, 'Just write out a card for him.'

'What is your name?'

'Return.'

Thinking I had not heard properly, I repeated, 'What, Return?'

'Yes, Return.'

I looked at the boss and again at the customer and we all laughed. The boss remarked, still laughing, 'So you return from the door to Return! Come and see if it is ready next week, eh?' he added to Return.

As I followed Return towards the door, I looked back at the boss seated, with his arms folded. Mr. Bloch's day started when he opened the doors at eight in the morning, and ended when we all left him sitting there, at the till, facing the door.

14
'Resign!'

THE BUSINESS of selling furniture and household appliances on hire purchase had been so successful that every day more shops were being opened in every town along the Reef. Furniture manufacturers were doing a booming business. There was keen competition to exploit the African buying power whose potential the manufacturers as well as the retailers were well aware of and could not ignore.

Thousands and thousands of cheap, mushroom-like brick or concrete structures were being built on the outskirts of every town to house the ever-increasing and inexhaustible numbers of the 'town' Africans.

In spite of their meagre earnings, they strove very hard to furnish these homes – a fact the manufacturers were well aware of. Their agents or salesmen daily scoured the locations and African townships, distributing pamphlets and encouraging black housewives to trade in their old furniture for new.

At Metropolitan Radio, coal stoves were being sold for little or no cash deposit at all if the prospective customers had old stoves, or anything else, to trade in. I remember one morning Mr. Bloch addressing a group of his salesmen who were about to 'invade' the townships. 'Accept anything for deposit, anything. An old chair, or a broom, an old bucket, anything. From those housewives who have nothing but children in their homes, you can take a child too as a trade-in for any goods she may want!'

Mr. Bloch had now bought another shop and another lorry to cope with the innumerable deliveries of all the branches. Daniel, another heavy-duty driver, was employed to assist Agrippa and Henry. Ever since Ricky, an expert salesman, had been engaged, there had been many more coal stoves going out. Johannes, our teaboy, was often called to assist with the loading of stoves and other goods.

When it was time for tea and the white staff were longing for it, Johannes's absence was felt.

On this particular day, two of Agrippa's 'lorry-boys' were absent from work. One was arrested, and the other was admitted to hospital with a serious stab wound in his chest. On such occasions, when Johannes was not in the shop, tea or coffee was ordered from the nearby tea-room – for the white staff only. The other staff would have to provide their own refreshment or do without.

But now Johannes would be absent for days and the coffee and tea was tapping more and more from the petty cash box, and Mr. Bloch was becoming concerned.

'Can't somebody make us tea here?' he asked.

Mrs. Kuhn replied, 'There's nobody. Adam is too busy watching the door and serving customers.'

'Nobody could drink Adam's tea, anyway. He doesn't know the meaning of cleanliness! Can't someone make us tea? How about you, Muriel?'

I was too offended to reply. Instead of employing another

tea-boy, the boss as usual was thinking of saving his money by using me. I sat thinking bitterly of all the different jobs I had had to 'help out' in because there was always a shortage, and it was being 'loyal to the firm', a thing which had created a gnawing feeling of guilt in me.

They picked on me because it was natural to them to do so. In the Republic of South Africa, the colour of your skin alone condemns you to a position of eternal servitude from which you can never escape. You cannot throw away the shackles no matter how hard you try. You are like the doormat. You are a *muntu*; your place is at the bottom of the ladder and there you must stay. You can never climb higher no matter what you do or what you have achieved.

'They asked me to make tea for them today at work,' I said to my husband at home that evening. Another man might have shrugged his shoulders and said, 'Oh well, you know what they are like. To avoid unpleasantness and keep your job, you'd better just make it for them.'

He did not say that. Instead he looked at me quickly and said sharply, 'No, you can't. You must resign. Give in your notice immediately!'

The answer came spontaneously like a natural reflex action to a painful stimulus. To him I was someone special in spite of being black. He spoke as if he had a goddess for a wife, not a mere black nanny. What right did he think he had to make such a decision, didn't he know that he was only a 'boy', and what right does a mere 'boy' have to be proud of anything – his parents, his wife, his children, what?

My husband was aware of all the repercussions yet he was willing to make the sacrifice. You don't often come across a type like him these days.

It just goes to show. Human beings are human beings and that's that. Some things you cannot destroy in any man. You may try to reduce him to the lowest levels but you cannot destroy him inside. A man will always fight for what he holds dear, and regards as his by right – his country, his wife, his children.

I took a pad and tried to scribble down the resignation letter. I knew it was not going to be easy. I wrote, 'Please accept my resignation ...'

That was no good, I decided, and tore away the first sheet. I began afresh. 'I hereby wish to inform you that I shall ...'

That was no good either, I thought, and tore out the second sheet. I faltered and hesitated. At last I said to my husband, 'I don't know what to say.'

'Let me see,' he said, taking the pad and pen from me. He came to my rescue. I read his draft and started again, copying it in my own handwriting:

'As a result of a very difficult decision I have had to make, I am obliged to tender herewith my resignation in good faith to you.

Will you, therefore, kindly regard this as due notice to allow me to terminate my services during this month of April.

I remain,

Yours faithfully,

...........................,'

Next morning I sat looking at the sealed envelope before me and thinking of what my husband had said to me before he left for work. 'Hand it in first thing.'

I was in a conflict. I just could not work. I had taken the envelope out of my bag and put it on my desk. Now that I *had* to hand the letter in, I was shaking and uncertain. My heart was beating hard. What would their reaction be?

I had made up my mind to hand the letter to Mrs. Kuhn rather than to Mr. Bloch. Somehow I felt that would be better.

Mr. Bloch called me to the other side to do the invoices as Mrs. Stein had not yet turned up for work. I felt this was the opportunity I had been waiting for. I put the letter on Mrs. Kuhn's desk and returned to occupy Mrs. Stein's place.

'What's this, Muriel?'

'A letter from me, Mrs. Kuhn,' I replied, feeling a little bolder. She opened it promptly. Hardly had she read it when she asked, looking at me and removing her reading glasses, 'But why?'

I did not answer but went on with my work. After I had finished, I took the invoice book, put it on Mr. Bloch's desk and went over to my own desk on the other side. I could feel Mrs. Kuhn's eyes following me.

'Won't you answer me, Muriel?' she asked in that motherly way of hers. There was a big lump in my throat which made it difficult for me to utter a single word.

After about half an hour, Mr. Bloch called me. He led the way towards the desk near where the bedroom suites were displayed. This meant that he wanted to speak in private without the fear of being overheard. He had my resignation letter in his hand, and waved it as he asked, 'Now tell me. What's all this about, what do you want?'

'I don't want anything. I just want to leave this very month, Mr. Bloch.'

'Why? Are you not satisfied? You are always smiling with all the customers and everybody likes you. When did we last give you an increment? If you want more money why don't you say so? What do you want?'

Mr. Bloch asked one question after another, giving me no chance to answer. When he had asked the last one and had apparently paused, I answered. 'I've *never* been given an increment! In any case, that is not why I want to leave, Mr. Bloch. I just want to go, that's all.'

'But why, why should you want to leave? You are healthy and fat. We all treat you well. What's wrong?'

Perhaps this was meant as a compliment but it made me get that 'white-master's-well-fed-dog' feeling again. I corrected him. 'I am fat because I eat the wrong type of food; not because I am happy.'

'Why, why are you unhappy? All right, Muriel, I'll tell you what I'll do. You've been with us nearly three years. I'll give you ten rands more per month. How's that, does that make you happy?'

'No, it doesn't.'

And I shook my head slowly, trying to show him that it was useless making any offers. How could I tell him that I was leaving because I did not want to make tea and be sent around to the cafés to buy refreshments for the white staff? None of them could understand it. What I was contemplating doing was totally out of key with the impression I had created in their minds.

I spared him the 'humiliation' of telling him that they had gone too far and were treating me with contempt. That soon he would be asking me to wash the floor like Johannes or to go and help carry the stoves. I thought of these things but I did not say them. I shook my head again. I had decided that I would not say anything except that I would like to leave.

What was the use of bickering with these people? All the altercation in the world could never knock sense into them.

You might as well be speaking to a wall. Their attitude is too old, centuries old.

He wrote the 'Ten rand per month increase' on the letter and gave it to me saying, 'Now take this back. *I* don't want it. Take it and speak to your husband. Go and do you work.'

I shook my head. It was no good. The additional crumbs he was now prepared to hand over to me would never be able to keep my happy. In any case, I was not leaving because of the inadequacy of my salary. I had seen what happened to all the other blacks. I had seen them standing there, on this side of the iron bars, looking hopefully towards the boss on pay day, sometimes even begging for more money. 'Just a few more cents, baas, please,' I would hear them pleading – all of them, agents, salesmen, drivers, mechanics, so-called lorry boys and shop-boys, store-room boys, etc. Some even resorted to tears. It broke my heart, and I had decided that I would never ask. I would go on accepting what they offered me without question. At least that would spare me the lamentation. What is the use of crying?

I moved slowly towards my desk, where I sat doing nothing. Mrs. Kuhn came over to me. She patted me on my shoulder and said softly, 'No, Muriel, you can't go. Just sit down and cool off. Do your work. I like you. I know we once quarrelled, but I like you. You can forgive and forget.'

When it was tea-time, Mrs. Kuhn ordered tea from Gants and – here came a shock – an extra cup for me. Imagine! This was to be the procedure in future whenever Johannes was not in the shop at tea-time. Thoughtfully I poured my cup into my own private cup, and sipped it from there.

15

Sophiatown

MRS. STEIN was worried and tired. She had no servant. The girl who had worked for her for a long time had been arrested for being without a permit to work in Johannesburg. She had been endorsed out, her pass was valid only for Rustenburg district and she and many others like her had been summarily removed under police escort back to their homes.

There were hundreds of servants available but most of those willing to work in the poorer suburbs were from the outside districts of the Transvaal and the other provinces; most were not resident or born in the urban areas. You could employ the so-called 'illegal' residents if you did not mind the risk of paying a heavy fine when you were found out.

'I could call back the girl I had before this one,' said Mrs. Stein. 'She's living in Johannesburg and she's got a permit. But she was so sulky and cheeky, though as far as cleanliness and housework were concerned, she was the best servant I've ever had.

'Oh, I'm so tired!' she went on. 'My husband feels so sorry for me, having to do all the housework during the weekend without any rest at all. He actually advised me to write to that cheeky girl and ask her to come back and work for us again.'

Mrs. Kuhn said decisively, 'I wouldn't take a girl back after I'd discharged her. She'd always think you couldn't do without her.'

Just then an African woman came in to pay. Mrs. Kuhn took her receipt book and looked at it. 'I see you last paid three months ago. Why?'

'I had no money. I have not been working. I'm looking for work.'

Mrs. Stein immediately looked up. She asked the customer, 'Can you do sleep-out work?'

'Yes, missus,' she replied, her face suddenly brightening.

'Where do you live?'

'In Fordsburg.'

'With your husband or boy-friend?'

'Yes, missus.'

'Can you be at Triomf every morning at seven o'clock?'

'Where is Trio, missus?'

'Not Trio, *Triomf*, near Newlands, just after you pass Westdene,' she said, pointing and directing.

But the girl's face was blank. She looked puzzled. Mrs. Stein tried harder.

'You know that Main road when you come from Brixton?'

The girl shook her head slowly. I could see that all the directing did not mean anything. I was bored and wanted to help.

'Ko Sophia,' I said. The girl looked from Mrs. Stein to me and back to her. Suddenly understanding, she said, 'Oh, *Sophia*! Why don't you just say Sophiatown, missus? I know Sophiatown very well. My uncle lived there long ago for a long time.'

The girl had got herself a job and it looked as if Mrs. Stein had got herself a clean-looking girl, although it was not for long, as usual.

Sophiatown – that beloved old Sophiatown – *our* Sophiatown. As students we used to refer to it proudly as 'the centre of the metropolis'. There are quite a few things for which I would never forgive the Nationalists, among them the forcible removal of Sophiatown. Ever since it was proclaimed a so-called 'black spot' and we were removed from there to Soweto, I had never been back to it. It had too many memories, happy as well as sad. I had always planned to go and have a look round some time. I had been told it was now transformed into a beautiful township for the lower income group whites. My visit there was, however, quite unplanned and accidental.

It was all thanks to Robert's reinstatement as an agent. He had returned to Metropolitan Radio after serving a five months' prison sentence for extortion. As he was an excellent salesman, Mr. Bloch was not reluctant to accept him back. Of course he had first sought the advice of the two good ladies who were always ready to play the role of business advisers.

'Well, you know Mr. Bloch, since William No. 1 left, you haven't really had a good "outside" salesman for furniture, stoves and other big items,' said Mrs. Stein.

'He is an expert salesman all right, but unfortunately you can't always trust him with money,' Mrs. Kuhn added. 'If only you could have somebody more reliable to go after him … Henry perhaps.'

'But Henry also "lost" a receipt book last month,' Mr. Bloch reflected thoughtfully. 'They are all such liars and tiefs,*

---

* Thieves.

man, you can't know. I'll have to send Henry after Robert, and then send somebody more reliable after Henry!'

Everybody laughed. Mrs. Stein then suggested, 'Why not send Muriel after Robert, Mr. Bloch?'

'That's a very good suggestion, Mrs. Stein. I wonder why I haven't thought of it before!'

And Mrs. Kuhn seconded the motion by saying, 'Yes, Henry can drive Muriel to Robert's customers.'

Robert visited the homes of his prospective customers during the day and helped them fill in particulars forms and sign the H.P. agreement forms, and submitted these to the office. Henry drove me to these homes in the afternoons and some evenings and Sunday mornings. I was to check and see whether Robert's sales were genuine or not. Wherever possible, I also collected money for deposits and issued receipts. If the customers did not have cash deposits, then trade-ins were accepted, as long as I thought the customers were 'good'.

Robert specialised in selling coal stoves. Old stoves were exchanged for new ones. This was considered a safe proposition because coal stoves could not be easily removed from one place to another like portable radios which Robert was said to have been giving away before he went to gaol. Yet they could be easily repossessed if the customer proved to be 'bad'.

So it was settled that I would go with Henry. I did not enjoy going out like that in the evenings, but it meant more money for me which I needed.

One afternoon I was waiting outside the shop for Henry by the van when he approached me and said, 'We've got to take Mrs. Stein to Sophiatown first, Muriel. She thinks her husband will be late coming for her tonight. I heard her ask Mr. Bloch to let her go off earlier with me today.'

'How will all three of us fit into the small front seat of the van, Henry?' I asked. 'I hope you are not thinking of making me sit outside on that open carrier.'

'No, of course not. If she doesn't want to wait for her husband and she is too lazy to walk to the bus stop after work, then she must just accept what I offer her.'

When Mrs. Stein came, I stood aside to see what would happen. She allowed me to go in first, saying that as she would be the first to be dropped, she might just as well sit nearest the door.

As we drove along, Henry said to me in vernacular, 'Why does she keep her face turned to the left, almost sticking through the open window?'

'I think she is trying very hard not to breathe the air inside the van with us. She wants to breathe the "free" air, and not the same air the kaffirs are breathing.' We both laughed.

The van moved on, down Main Road, from Westdene – past First Gate in Western Native Township, then past Toby Street, the first street in Sophiatown. It was moving through the old familiar places. I felt like reaching out and touching them. The van turned right into Tucker Street, and stopped suddenly. Mrs. Stein said, pointing to the left, 'This is where I live, Muriel.'

I was not listening, I was thinking. Just a few yards further up, I was led out of my uncle's home to the African Methodist Episcopal Church as a young bride, happy and full of hopes for the future. I alighted and moved slowly up to the corner of Victoria Road and Good Street. The partially demolished walls of the church still stood there, the words 'God Our Father, Christ Our Redeemer, Man Our Brother' still legible beneath the painted crucifix.

As an infant, you are christened in church, brought up in a Christian home and you acquire some education. Later, as you grow older, you are joined in holy matrimony to the man or woman of your choice. Together, you in turn build a home full of hope for the future. But the truth begins to stare you in the face. Life is not what it should be. After marriage you do *not* live happily ever after. You shudder at the thought of bringing into this world children to be in the same unnatural plight as yourself, your parents and your grandparents before you – passing on a heritage of serfdom from one generation to another. You are not human. Everything is a mockery.

I stood and looked into the past which had held hopes of redemption. I stood and listened. It was not the sound of the passing traffic that I was hearing, nor was it the shrill screams and laughter of the barefoot white youngsters kicking a ball from one to another. It was the rich voices of people all standing with their right thumbs pointing upwards, singing with stern faces, people young and old, of all races, hoping for redemption.

A woman's clear high-pitched voice led the multitude in a beautiful soprano solo – appealing, entreating, pleading, praying …

'*Mabayeke!* … (Let them leave …)

Then followed the rich contralto, tenor and bass, repeating the haunting and demanding words:

'*Mabayek'umhlaba Wethu!* (Let them leave our land …)

'*Thina Sizwe … Thina Sizwessinsundu* (We the black nation …)

'*Sikalela … Sikalela Izwe Lethu!* (We weep for our country…)

'*Elathathwa …*

'*Elathathwa Ngambamhlophe* (which was taken by the whites …)

'*Mabayeke* …

'*Mabayek'umhlaba Wethu!* (Let them leave our land alone!)'

The voices resounded the demand; the music rising into a beautiful, sad and piercing crescendo.

My mind recalled the events of that fateful week, when all efforts to resist the removal had failed. The women's section of the now banned African National Congress decided that on the Sunday before the day or the removal, all women and children should hold a prayer meeting on the Freedom Square. They knelt there praying to our forefathers – the gods of Africa – they sang 'freedom' songs of hope, surrounded as usual by the inevitable circle of the constabulary, others taking notes in plain clothes. I looked at the *koppie** where the tears of the African women and children soaked deep into the soil. I do not think they will ever dry. They have built their 'Triomf' on top of them. Whether they have triumphed or not, time alone will tell.

The next day, Sophiatown was virtually under siege. The residents were finally removed under police escort. All the pavements were lined with heavily armed police of all colours from all over the Republic. There was practically no resistance, how could there be? Father Huddleston and the African leaders there were removed to the nearby Newlands police station.

When the people and their belongings had been removed, the bulldozers moved in like tanks, destroying, smashing, razing, reducing everything to ruin. All around was dust, heaps of dirty bricks, soot and rubble …

Henry's voice brought me back from the past. 'What do you think you are doing, how long are you going to stand there admiring the beautiful European houses?'

---

* hillock. (Afrikaans)

'If you only knew, Henry. I never even saw these houses; all I "saw" was our own homes – the poor old so-called "slum structures". Don't you know the expression "a poor thing but mine own"?'

We moved away. He asked, 'What do they call this place now – Triom?'

'Triomf. Do you know what that means, Henry? It is a Dutch word meaning "triumph" in English. When you have finally succeeded in getting your enemy to go down on his knees before you, or you have at last knocked him out and he lies there on the ground, sprawled and defeated, then you have triumphed. Hence the Nationalists have triumphed over us.'

'What the hell, what triumph?' said Henry. 'All those cockroaches and lice they have built their beautiful homes on … where is their pride? All those nice gardens of theirs fertilised by the shit of black children who used to run about here naked and neglected while their mothers cared for white kids. All those buckets from the latrines they used to empty into the streets – where's all their white pride?'

Henry cursed and swore and worked himself into such a state that his whole body was shaking. He fumbled in his pocket for a cigarette, and put it between his wet lips. He lighted it, puffed and burst into a dreadful fit of coughing, rocking violently until the sweat came running down his forehead and temples.

'Why don't you stop smoking?' I said. 'You know that your chest is not so good. What about that spot on your lung? What good does it do to get in such a state?'

He did not reply. He drove on until we reached Soweto.

16
The passport

ONE MONDAY just before lunch, Mrs. Kuhn said to no-one in particular, 'I must say I prefer to do the entering than to sit at the till and write out receipts. But I wish we filed the cards according to the customers' first names. They are easier to spell than those terrible surnames. It's the *hunting* for the cards that I can't stand!'

'But they have such funny first names,' said Mrs. Stein.

Mrs. Kuhn smiled.

'Yes, names like Lorry and Spitfire ... or Capetown. Lovey, Beauty, Naughty-boy ... those you can always spell easily.'

'But some of them make me laugh,' said Mrs. Stein. 'Imagine naming your child Ostrich or Sprikaan or Oor! I mean, Sprikaan means locust and Oor means Ear ... I mean, really!'

It was funny and none of us could help laughing. Mrs. Stein asked me from the other side, 'Muriel, why do the natives like to give their children such funny names? We have Oneboy, Spirit ...'

'I don't know why, Mrs. Stein. I suppose they just take a fancy to a word and then they name their child that. Oneboy could mean that the parents had a number of girls one after another, and then they got a boy.'

Douglas was standing near the heater at the bottom of the stairs next to my desk listening to the conversation.

Mrs. Kuhn sniggered. 'But just think of Caramel Toffee ...'

'And Neverdie. We had a Neverdie, too,' said Mrs. Stein.

'Yes, and a Looseboy!'

'So I think we have had everything – sweets, spirits, animals, insects and fruits.'

'Fruits?' asked Mrs. Kuhn.

'Yes, we had a Banana.'

'Of course, Banana. He is always coming to pay with his employer. The two are inseparable.'

'And what about the other one I saw the other day. I don't know what language it is – Ayisiyu, or something. Muriel, what's that now?' asked Mrs. Stein.

'Oh yes. That must be "I see you," hey, Muriel?' said Mrs. Kuhn.

They all laughed.

'No, Mrs. Kuhn,' I said. 'You see, I asked that customer what her name meant and she said that it was actually the initials "I.C.U." Her father used to be an official of an organisation called Industrial Commercial Workers' Union at the time she was born. She says the clerks at the pass-office did not understand what she said when they made her pass, so they just wrote Ayisiyu.'

'So you could name a child UNO,' said Douglas.

'Or TATA,' I said.

'What's that mean?' asked Douglas.

'The Transvaal African Teachers' Association. I.C.U. was the first African Trade Union movement, formed in about 1918 by a man called Kadalie, I think.'

'You know the one I could never stop laughing at,' said Mrs. Stein, 'was the one called Willem Draaghoender. I could never attend to him, I used to laugh so much. And what's more, he used to live in Kak Street, Newclare. Is there such a street, Douglas?'

'Yes, there is, Mrs. Stein.'

In the thick of it, when everybody was enjoying laughing at all the funny names, the postman walked in carrying a very big bag slung over his shoulder. He removed the heavy laces of the bag from around his shoulder and put it down near the secondhand radiograms. He went to the counter and started sorting the letters. He smiled amicably, tilting his brown cap slightly – a sign of respect for the white lady. He said, 'Good afternoon, madam, the post is a little late today. We are very short-staffed at our branch.'

'Don't tell me you have the same problem that we have here.'

Although he was a Coloured man, the white women always used to speak to him politely.

'Are you bringing us a lot of registered post?'

'Yes, lots and lots of it, madam.'

When Mrs. Kuhn had finished signing for all the registered letters, the postman opened his cumbersome bag, containing parcels of different sizes. He also looked at some of them, putting each one on the radiogram and apparently sorting them out.

'Adam, there are customers at the door,' said Douglas.

Then he winked at the postman who slung his heavy bag over his shoulder. Douglas climbed the stairs.

After a time Douglas came down the stairs, smiling and throwing a ball of twine into the air and catching it. He said, 'Now she can have her twine back. It has done its work.'

He deposited the roll on the counter. I had not taken too much notice when he had borrowed it earlier that day. Now I did notice how cheerful he looked. He went out whistling a tune happily. He came back soon afterwards with a cold drink and a sandwich, stood near to the heater and started eating.

'One thing about this place,' he said, 'is that although the boss is stingy, *daar is daarem brood hier.*'*

He smiled and gulped down the cold drink.

'Douglas, what do you mean by that?' I said.

'The government won't do anything to help me, and you didn't take up that proposition I made to you, so I make my own ... what do you call them? ... my own fringe benefits.'

'I still don't understand you, Douglas.'

He spoke softly.

'The postman and I have a little deal on.'

'Deal?'

'Yes.'

'But you never went near that postman, Douglas. What could he have done for you?'

'He went out of here carrying in his bag four lovely portable radios and a chassis, all neatly wrapped up in a parcel of brown paper and twine addressed to an imaginary recipient. And to think that all of it was done easily here ... under your eyes ...'

'And ...?'

'And he and I split the proceeds. Clever, eh?'

---

* 'There is, notwithstanding, "bread" in this place.' (Afrikaans)

17

My mother's beckoning voice

MRS. STEIN looked through the steel bars into the unusually beautiful black face of an African woman, who was taking a receipt book out of her bag.

'What do you want, Nanny?'

The African woman did not seem impressed by the white lady's kind manner. She replied bluntly, 'Don't call me Nanny. *Your* Nanny is looking after your kids at your house.'

"But I don't know your name.'

'You don't need to know my name to speak to me. I don't know yours either, but you wouldn't allow me to call you Nanny, would you?'

The cashier sighed heavily and raised her eyebrows as she turned slightly to look at her white colleagues. On her way out, the customer met Adam and asked him, 'Why do you people write ugly letters to customers even when we let you know we cannot pay, and ask you to give us a chance?'

'Did you receive a letter, my sister?' Adam asked innocently.

'Yes.'

Adam shrugged his shoulders, and gave way to her as she passed out into the street. Then he laughed quietly.

Meanwhile Mrs. Stein was expressing her annoyance. 'I get so mad when they are like that! Try to be nice to them and they give you a slap in the face.'

'She thought she was somebody with all that horrible make-up and lipstick on her face,' agreed Mrs. Kuhn.

By the time the next black customer stood at the counter and gazed with her black face through the bars, the white women had agreed that they were sick of cheeky ungrateful natives.

When Ethel Sibanda's receipt book showed that she had last paid three months ago Mrs. Stein said loudly, 'Here's another one – last paid three months ago.'

She stood up sharply from her chair and went to the Inside Sales tray but she could not find the card. She asked the customer curtly, 'Did you buy from the shop or outside?'

'Outside.'

'Who sold it to you?'

The customer could not remember the salesman's name but she tried to describe him. Mrs. Stein looked for the card again and found it. She said to me, 'She hasn't paid since she bought the stove. That receipt must be the cash receipt for the deposit. Tell her to wait for Mr. Bloch.'

I was feeling guilty. In the previous week, I had taken over from Mrs. Stein as credit control manager. I had been instructed to continue sending out letters from where she had left off. I had sent out hundreds of them, from the Ns to the Zs. For those customers who I thought should receive a letter, I had been faced with the difficult task of deciding what letter to send. There were five different varieties before we got to the more demanding and more threatening 'green letter' and the 'personal summons'.

The boss had said to me, 'Just send them letters, Muriel; send them letters. Where a customer has been sent a ten-day letter and has not paid, send a personal summons, or a green letter – anything.' Of course the boss knew that he could issue such instructions only in the case of non-white customers.

Being the letter-writer was the one duty I had feared most. I had seen how customers would come in furiously demanding to see the credit control manager 'in person'. And I had heard them storm out of the shop cursing and threatening. I dreaded to think what would happen to me and my family in Soweto (where taking life means nothing), if it were to be known that I was responsible for the letters.

The complaining customers were wisely told that the Credit Control Department offices were 'in town'. But that did not make me feel better. I used to have spasms in my stomach through fright.

There was a lowering of tones among the waiting customers as Mr. Bloch walked in with a traveller, smiling and talking. He took out a small portable radio from the glass showcase and gave it to the traveller, who was presumably summing up their talk.

'Yes Larry, they're lucky their father was born before them. If they were born before their father, there wouldn't be all that. One son brought a Mustang from America the other day – a fabulous thing! The other is moving in a huge Jag. They're secure. Their children, their children's children, will be secure for generations to come. That's the thing about money. You must just remember to choose the right parents!'

The telephone rang and Mrs. Stein called out, 'It's for you, Mr. Bloch.'

.'Who is it?'

'It's Mr. Skinner, your lawyer.'

'Who?'

Mrs. Stein must have remembered that the boss's hearing had been unreliable of late, for she shouted more loudly, 'Mr. Paul Skinner, Mr. Bloch.'

'Not Paul Kruger?' the boss shouted back, smiling. The traveller laughed, patted him on the shoulder, and said, 'All right, Larry, I'll be seeing you. Thanks for the present for my daughter.' And he went off with the portable radio.

The boss took the receiver and sat down near the switchboard. Speaking to his lawyers about his firms might take a long time. He just forgot about the waiting customers, especially when they were black.

'Yes ... Yes ... And you know what, the land transactions have paid me more than I worked for in forty years. They are worth far more than this furniture-selling business here. Ag, man, you never see the money. It's all tied up in the books and stock ... The value of land never goes down, it always rises ... It always pays you in the end. In fact, the longer you wait, the more it pays you ... The Swaziland one? ... it's approximately three thousand acres. One thousand agricultural and two thousand mountainous ... There's very good soil with plenty of water all the year round ... natural fountains all over. Three hundred acres of planted gum trees, ready for cutting. Who wants it? What, a *soggadika?** Where can he get all that money from? ... N-no man ... I want twenty thousand rands for that farm ... N-n-no. What he offers I can get from selling the trees only, and I'll still have the farm ... What do you think? Should I sell? ... What do you think independence will mean? ...

* Variant of *soggen* (see page 123).

Should I get back my money and back out? … I think the *soggens* there are friendlier than here, if you ask me. O.K., … you just keep trying, we shall see.'

Mr. Bloch looked round him uneasily. Too many were waiting for him. But as soon as he replaced the receiver, another call came in.

'What, what? Who? … Oh, Muriel, just find out what this boy wants, man. He sounds like he is crying.'

It was the old story. It was old Simon Tlebere. He wanted to know why we had sent him a letter. His card revealed that he had the habit of skipping in between payments. Also, instead of paying the stated instalment of nine rands per week, he was only paying five. I had sent him a 'final warning' letter. I asked Simon Tlebere to hold on, and explained to the boss these details. I was still doing that softly, when Mrs. Stein asked me, 'Who is it, Muriel, Simon Tlebere?'

'Yes, Mrs. Stein.'

'Did you send him a letter?'

'Yes. A "final warning". I noticed that he was in arrears but had not been sent a letter.'

'You should not have sent him a letter.'

'Why not?' the boss asked her.

'Because *you* allowed him to pay half the instalment, Mr. Bloch. Don't you remember that grey-haired old boy who came with a letter from the hospital to say that he has T.B.?'

'Oh yes, now I remember. All right, Muriel, tell him it's all right. Tell him the letter was sent by mistake.'

Only Mrs. Stein could remember the verbal agreement between the boss and the customer. She had not bothered to make a note of it on the card. She had perhaps not realised the necessity to do so when she could keep it 'in her head'. But how was I to know what was in her head? Fortunately Simon Tlebere had not come to the shop personally with the letter, or I might never have lived to tell the tale.

Rebecca Nkosi had nudged her way impatiently through the other customers who had been waiting longer. She looked like an amazon, with her voluminous bosom as she stood dominating the scene and holding bank-notes in her hand. If it had not been for those notes, someone might have told her to stand back and wait her turn.

'Who's who, now, here?' asked the boss, looking at the many black faces through the bars. He noticed the money in Rebecca's hand and asked, 'What does *she* want?'

'She wants to know how much you charged for the repair to her radiogram. The invoice has not been sent yet, but she wants to pay now. But Ethel Sibanda there came long ago, Mr. Bloch, she should be attended to first.'

Ethel Sibanda produced from somewhere under her dress a crumpled statement, which she put on the counter in front of the boss. Mr. Bloch looked at the paper without touching it. He said, 'That's yours, not mine. Why are you giving it to me? Keep it in between your breasts, it's quite safe there.'

The customer laughed.

'The agent told me to wait and not pay till I get letter, master. I wait, I wait, now I get this letter. It say, "You are behind the area – twenty rands". Why? Who say I owe money?'

'You have *arrears* of twenty rands, not "area". That agent told you lies if he *did* tell you not to pay for three months.'

'Who hired the agent, me or you?' Ethel asked, determined to hold her ground.

'I did, but ...'

'Well, why do you hire somebody you don't trust? He must pay the areas, not me.'

'I don't think you want the stove. You go and cook outside in the street in a paraffin tin. I'll take back my stove and
you can come and pick up your old one. It's in the yard; not
even worth ten shillings. I want money, not talk, talk, talk!'

Rebecca Nkosi, standing next to Ethel and looking askance
at her, fanned her sweaty brow with the bank-notes impatiently.
She rolled her big eyeballs from Ethel to the boss, nodding her
head in approval of his firmness. She said, 'Yes, baas, you're
right. Money talk. *Kukulumimali!* ... Money talk!'

I put Rebecca's old card on the counter. The boss looked
at it. It showed a credit balance of twenty rands.

'All right, Rebecca, you can pay your five rands and go. I
can see it's becoming too hot for you here. Now, who's next?'

The telephone rang again, and Mr. Bloch complained,
'That telephone just never stops ringing. It's terrible, man.'

Mrs. Stein answered it. 'Muriel, it's for you. A trunk call
from ... I don't know where – an African name. Go and pick
up that receiver on your desk, quick!'

A trunk call for me? It must be my mother, I thought, as I
picked up the receiver, my heart pounding like a hammer. It
was indeed Mmè's voice. I could never mistake it for anybody
else's. I was overjoyed. Her voice sounded so near even though
she was six hundred miles away. I felt an overwhelming desire
to extend my hand and touch her.

'Muriel, you are well? And the children?'

'Mmè, Mmè, how good ...'

'Are you still wasting your time in that shop, my daughter? When are you going to start thinking seriously about your
future, the future of your children? All the education I worked
hard to give you has meant nothing.'

'I have to earn my living, Mmè ...'

163

'I would sooner have you selling cakes than sitting in there and asking for people's passes. There is no hope for you there. You will never be able to do anything for yourself ...'

Long after I had replaced the receiver, my mother's voice echoed in my ears like the voice of my own conscience, sounding a warning, reaching out to wrench me from some imminent calamity.

To Mmè, this country had gone from bad to worse. When Lesotho had finally been granted independence, she had decided to go and settle there permanently. To her, it had been like fleeing from Egypt to Canaan. Lesotho's self-government she saw as a kind of redemption.

Mmè's stubborn lack of interest whenever people spoke of the politics of the Republic of South Africa troubled me. She would snap irritably, 'Yes, yes, I know all about it; the meetings, the strikes, which always end in the shooting of innocent people, the struggles, the passive resistances, the bannings and banishments ... I know all about it ... How many times have I told you how hard we used to try back in the nineteen-twenties?'

Then when she had asked that question, she would stare blankly into space, and I would know that she had let a shutter descend over her ears. It did not matter to Mmè that Lesotho was only a small fraction of the vast black continent. She could not see that the destiny of the one million Basotho would always be intermingled with that of the teeming millions of voiceless, helpless races surrounding them, that no protective moat could ever be built round Lesotho. It was pointless to try and speak to Mmè. All she wanted to do was to redeem her own; to grab me to safety before I too, sank in the quicksand with all the others. The Republic was beyond redemption.

I was left feeling restless and frustrated. Mmè was right. What prospects did the future hold for me anyway? One thing was certain. I would have to leave. To go on working at Metropolitan Radio would be torture. Every time I was forced to be 'loyal to the firm' I would get those cramps deep down in my entrails. Every time I asked for a customer's pass book, I would feel like a policeman, who, in this country, is the symbol of oppression. I would continue to feel like a traitor, part of a conspiracy, a machinery deliberately designed to crush the soul of a people.

To a person without reasoning powers, Metropolitan Radio was a wonderful place. I could go on working there as long as I wanted. But I would have to give my best and receive very little in return. My presence would be felt but never recognised, let alone rewarded. I would have to remain static, junior, for the rest of my working life, irrespective of my experience and my proficiency, a shock absorber, ready to be used on demand. I would literally have to trample on my conscience, to gobble it up (as we say in our language). Every time a black customer paid more than he was supposed to, I would have to keep quiet 'in loyalty to the firm'.

I could go on working, earning perhaps a few more rands than now. As the years went by, and the company grew bigger and richer, and more 'girls' were employed, I would very likely be promoted to a 'boss-girl' just as Adam now claimed to be 'boss-boy'. When I grew too old to work (and had joined the ranks of the so-called 'unproductive labour') I would be advised to retire with a gold watch, in recognition of my long, loyal service, to some Basotho tribal Bantustan and left there to sit in the sun, waiting for the end to come. And when the end did come at last, perhaps my relatives would be given a coffin

165

– by the company I served so well – in which to bury my remains: a tribute to a good and faithful servant.

How long I had been sitting there, I do not know. It could have been a matter of a few minutes. but when I awoke from my reverie, it was as if I had been away from the shop for hours. Mr. Bloch was still busy with his customers. There was one who maintained that he had been cheated into agreeing to purchase goods. Glaring at the boss through the steel bars, he demanded, 'Why is it so much?'

'That is interest. The interest covers you for two years. I know you people. Sometimes you come in to say that you are out of work or sick. Or maybe you just take a little more time to pay.'

'One of these days these boys of yours will die. They think they can come and humbug us. Why don't they tell us all this before we buy? You give us things which kill us.'

The customer obviously realised that he had accepted a Trojan horse. Adam, in his loyalty to the firm, tried to pacify him. 'My friend, stop fighting. Listen to me. Those agents are just like a man making love to a young lady. Everything is made to look rosy … he promises anything …'

I wondered why Adam never realised that by saying that, he was actually aggravating the situation, that he was admitting that the customer was cheated. Yet he always said the same thing. I am certain that if he had said it in English, the boss would shut him up. Anyway, the customers always felt even more offended, and the whites on the other side would never understand why because the argument between Adam and the customers would be carried on in vernacular. This particular customer reacted sharply. He nearly pushed Adam away. He shouted, 'Don't talk to me about girls and making love. You're one of the old people who are scared of Europeans. I'm not scared of them! You only want your children to be healthy and fat, and ours to be lean. I've dealt with you whites for a long time; I know you!'

'Your old stove is still in the yard. If you don't want my stove I can come and pick it up and return your old one,' retorted the boss.

'I don't want to see your dirty boys in my house again. I don't want collectors. I'll come and pay myself here *if* I decide to keep the thing at all.'

The boss looked at the infuriated customer as he stalked out.

'Every one of them is a politician these days, man. Anyway, that's the only way to make them pay. You stop writing and they sit down and don't pay.'

He asked me to make a note on the customer's card that the account must be watched. I wrote on the card WATCH THIS A/C in bold letters.

The boss went over to the switchboard and dialled a number.

'Hallo, Charlie, how are you? ... Are you going to *shul?* All right, I'll pick you up tonight at six ...'

So, I thought, the Jews are going to gather in their synagogue to worship. They are going to ask God to make them rich and powerful – and good luck to them. Perhaps it is high time we, too, went on our knees and prayed God to grant us that boldness, unintimidated by fear, to stand up against those things that we believe are not right – and to suffer the consequences.

18

'This is home!'

I WAS startled, and nearly jumped out of my skin when a male voice behind me suddenly said, 'Hallo, Muriel!'

I looked up quickly into Douglas's bloodshot eyes. It was the first time he had paid a friendly visit to Metropolitan Radio since he had left over three months earlier. I could see that he had had far too much to drink. He was finding it difficult to keep his balance even on both legs. He steadied himself with his arm against the back of my chair. 'Hallo, stranger!' I said jokingly. 'You promised me you would come and repair my radio but you never came.'

'I'm coming, man, don't worry. Where's the boss?'

'He's gone down to his store-rooms. Are you working?'

'No. Why should I work?'

'How do you live; your children, your wife?'

'I get unemployment pay. I just sit and drink.'

'So I see. But unemployment pay is only about a third of what you used to earn, isn't it? Or are you doing repairs privately at home?'

'No. I want to get my heavy-duty driver's licence. There's

a job waiting for me at Putco (meaning Public Utility Transport Co-operation).'

'I don't think there's *brood* (bread) there.'

We both laughed.

'No, not like here, but they pay well.'

I noticed that he had lost a lot of weight and had more streaks of grey in his hair. I felt sorry for him.

'Wouldn't you like to come back here?' I asked. 'After all you're used to this place. You've been here for years. Why did you leave anyway?'

'Because I was fed up, man. All those lies that Boer at the back there next to our yard told Mr. Bloch about me jumping into the yard after hours and stealing parts out of the old radios there.'

'All right, but it was your word against the Boer's. Mr. Bloch only asked you if you knew anything about the missing parts and told you what that Boer had told him. He didn't fire you.'

'That fool, Lennie, must have said something too. Why did they suddenly decide to fit wire mesh on the attic window overlooking the yard? He must have told the boss that I used to lower small portables through there. I didn't like feeling I was being watched.'

'Yes, well, sometimes I remember that "passport" affair. Putting wrapped and addressed parcels in the old radiograms and letting the postman collect them – that was brilliant. But sometimes I used to worry that the boss would look at the radios displayed on the window sill and ask, "What's happened to that radio that used to be there?".'

Douglas laughed, but something told me he would still like to come back to Metropolitan Radio. Looking for work in Johannesburg can be really frustrating. It is very difficult to find work where your experience will be taken into consideration. Even if you are an expert, employers always stress the fact that you are not a 'licence holder' and therefore not entitled to enjoy the privileges of a skilled or semi-skilled worker. This makes it easier or 'legal' for them to pay you as little as they like.

Someone might accuse me of being a party to the making of *brood* which Douglas used to indulge in so frequently, because I kept my mouth shut about it. Maybe I was an accomplice because I kept quiet. But I felt very little guilt. What I feared most was what I knew would happen to Douglas and his family if he was found out. I was not there to spy on anyone.

Taking those portables from a man like Mr. Bloch who had all the laws in his favour to protect him and his descendants for all time, and to provide for their security, well-being and comfort, would never compare with the suffering which was reflected all over Douglas's face even as he stood there trying to force a smile.

I said, 'Do ask if you can come back. He'll take you back. You used to be his best mechanic, as he himself often used to say.'

'Who does the repairs now?'

'What Lennie can't manage, he sends to the store to be repaired there by those assemblers of his. *Do* come back,' I urged again.

'You speak like Agrippa. I know he has been taken back, fired and hired again, all because he can repossess people's goods better than anybody else. He's got no feelings, that Agrippa. When I asked him why he keeps coming back after he has been kicked out, he says proudly, "This is home! *Kusekaya lapha* – this is home. I am back home!" No wonder Mr. Bloch thinks he is God.'

Douglas's tongue, always ready to lash out against Lennie at the slightest provocation, was now even more venomous and unrestrained. He recalled all the 'atrocities' which the white mechanic had committed and related them with no fear of being overheard on the other side.

'All he ever used to do was to ask me to get him Coloured and African girls.'

'What? A *herenvolk** like him?'

'You don't know anything. He used to beg me to get him *our* girls. Didn't you always see him sitting at his bench looking at the photos of the Coloured and African women in the *Post*?'

'Does he buy the *Post*?'

'No. But when I bought it, he'd always steal it. He's a bloody hypocrite, like all of them. You know, he begged me for Mavis's address.'

I remembered Mavis vividly. She had a figure most women would envy and she moved gracefully. Besides being naturally beautiful, Mavis was very sophisticated. She had warmth and personality.

'He offered to pay me two rands if I got her address.'

'How would you do that?'

'I would arrange for a false radio check-up, and then we would call there. I would wait in the van outside and keep watch, that's all. With her, the snag was that she was working at a flat in town where there were too many eyes.'

'Have you done that before? I mean, where there are not so many eyes?'

'Oh yes! Many times. All I had to do was tell whoever he fancied about the white mechanic's feelings, and then if she was

---

* the chosen people, the people of God. (Afrikaans)

agreeable, I just used to leave them in the house and sit in the van outside.'

Douglas laughed mischievously.

'It paid both of us, you see. He got what he wanted, and I got the money.'

I felt sorry for Douglas. He was trying hard to pretend that everything was all right, yet it was obvious that he was unhappy.

'Douglas, if you had the necessary documents and enough money, perhaps you would open up your own radio repair shop in any location and be your own boss, wouldn't you?'

'I certainly would. Like Peter Kahn. He's opened his own shop. Well, his father is wealthy and of course he's got the certificate because he's white. You know, he wanted me to go and work with him and he said he'd let me know, but he hasn't. He's scared of employing me, I think.'

Up to now Adam had avoided coming over to us. He had only been casting casual glances at us and smiling. Douglas now jerked a finger at him and said contemptuously, 'For him as well as Agrippa, this is home. Adam will only leave here when he's a corpse. Where can he go to? He is a "foreign native", a Rhodesian. He has to remain tied to Mr. Bloch for the rest of his life like a slave; he has been sold to him and may not leave him for another master. At least I'm free!'

And Douglas left.

19

The final kick

WHEN JOHANNES had left for a job which paid him a few cents more, it had not been difficult to replace him with another tea-boy. Adam had recommended Jonas, another so-called 'foreign native' who had been born in Rhodesia, like Adam himself.

Mr. Bloch's sister, Mrs. Kuhn, had encouraged him to engage Jonas because such foreign 'boys' were better than the Johannesburg-born *tsotsis* who were untrustworthy, cheeky and had the bad habit of always demanding more money.

Six years earlier, Jonas's pass had been confiscated and he had been given seventy-two hours to leave South Africa. But Jonas had remained, evading the police and working at different places. Jonas had become a man in fear, living on borrowed time. The fear of arrest had now become an obsession. A slight twist of luck against him might mean serving a prison term, after which he would be summarily removed under police escort, and be deposited at the nearest point in his 'native' land.

He viewed every strange white man with suspicion, fearing to hear the words, *'Waar is jou Pas?'* (Where is your pass?) On several occasions, when he saw an officious-looking European walk in, he would call me to the kitchen and ask me, 'Did white man ask who works here, is he a detective?' I would laugh it off, but it was pathetic rather than amusing for a man to live like that for so many years.

Jonas could never look anyone straight in the face, particularly a white person. Once Mrs. Stein asked me, 'Muriel, why does that Jonas look away or at the floor when one speaks to him? Is it because he's being respectful? I wonder why he's always so shifty.'

I felt like saying 'You too would be like that if you were in his boots, wouldn't you? But I didn't. You can think what you like, but you may not say what you like to a white person. Not if you are black, and want to keep your job.

Yet among the African labourers in the vicinity of Metropolitan Radio, Jonas was revered. Just as witch-doctors were respected in the olden days because they were said to wield superhuman powers, Jonas too commanded respect, almost fear, as a witch-doctor. This art, Adam claimed, Jonas had inherited from his father, who had been a formidable, highly successful and popular medicine-man in Rhodesia. The African labourers consulted Jonas who helped them time and again with their ailments and other problems. They attributed his astounding success in evading the long arm of the Nationalist law to his highly effective drugs and *muti** which, they believed, made him invisible whenever he was confronted by a policeman or a so-called 'police-boy' during pass raids.

At Metropolitan Radio, Jonas earned himself even greater honour by the manner in which he had saved Agrippa from certain dismissal many times. Especially the last time.

---

* potion or 'stick' for healing; something a medicine man or doctor would give a patient to cure an ailment. (Nguni)

Things looked really bad. The atmosphere at Metropolitan Radio was tense. The boss was in a bad mood. For the third day now, Agrippa had not reported for work, with the lorry and all.

'Adam!' the boss shouted.

'Yes, baas,' Adam answered from somewhere near the door.

'Where is he? Oh, he's still standing there with the feather-duster. Oh man, *that* bloke! I tell you he's *ower* the wall; he's too old, man. Takes two portables to the window and stays there with them.'

On his way, as he came towards the counter, the boss was passed by Mrs. Stein who was rushing out to the chemist.

'Where's she off to now, Lieda?'

'Chemist,' Mrs. Kuhn replied impatiently.

'Honestly! There's always something. Either chemist or crackers or something. Always. The machine is standing still, the accounts are not out, invoices are not completed, customers haven't received letters for two months now. Honestly, man, I can't take it! What about the shortage, Lieda? Has she found the missing ten rands?

'And where's Agrippa? That one is a waste of time. He's a criminal. Twice I had to pay fines to release him from gaol, arrested for reckless driving, three times he was led out of here in handcuffs for ignoring summonses and the deliveries had to be delayed for days. And then he has the nerve to stay away with my lorry and lorry-boys for four days! I tell you, I'd like to kick him from here to … to … to Jerusalem, man!'

Mrs. Kuhn, who had not taken the boss seriously, and had continued to add up figures in her books, replied, without looking up, 'Well, I told you, Larry; get more staff, *reliable* staff. I tell you, Muriel,' she added, turning to me, 'never work for relations. They always expect you to do more work, they expect more and more out of you.'

Late in the afternoon Agrippa arrived with his boys and the lorry loaded to capacity with repossessed goods.

'Agrippa, you've been away four days, with my lorry and my boys. Saturday, Sunday, Monday and now Tuesday – four days. Go and load off those goods at the store and come back and give me my keys. I don't want to see you again!'

'Why do you count Saturday and today, baas? I'm here to-day. Saturday I went away to make deliveries at two o'clock and I only finish Sunday, baas. Yesterday I was doing repossess. You know sometimes I wait until they go to work and then I get a chance to go in their house and take the goods. You think is easy to get the goods, baas?'

Mr. Bloch was looking at the fully-loaded lorry, thinking. He went out to where it was parked and checked the mileage. He came back fuming with fury, his eyes bloodshot, and his flaccid dewlap sweaty. He bellowed, 'He must have been to Swaziland or driving up and down to all the shebeens in the locations all these days with my lorry. He's done enough mileage to travel to … to … to the *moon*, man!'

Agrippa was worried now. When things looked really bad, and he feared he had really had it, he used to consult Jonas to help him ward off the evil spirits which had gone into the boss.

Jonas used to give him a piece of stick to chew and say, 'Now go and speak to the boss, or just stand near him and look at him. Go!'

'I'm definitely dismissing him!' the boss went on muttering to himself as he checked the crumpled, greasy, dirty and sometimes bloodstained copies of delivery notes which Agrippa had given him.

Like everybody else, I had grown to accept it as a fact that Mr. Bloch would never sack Agrippa. I remembered the many times this sort of scene had been re-enacted and yet Agrippa continued to work at Metropolitan Radio. Nobody sympathised with Agrippa, neither white nor black staff. Almost all the blacks would look on helplessly at the struggling Mr. Bloch and remark, 'But this is too much, man. This Agrippa has gone too far.' Yet Mr. Bloch showed more patience than I thought any white person could with a black.

The whole thing would always end up the same way. The white staff would once more be disappointed, disgusted and disillusioned. The boss could not be trusted; he was not a man of his word; he was weak and unpredictable. It would always end up with Lieda remembering how her brother had failed to kick out Adam, the salesman who had actually implied that *she* was a thief – that insult to her character and integrity for which she would never forgive him. Mrs. Stein would recall bitterly the Hudson affair, when that black salesman had claimed that she was stupid, and had better go back to school. She would recall how she had spent hours and hours crying, unable to sleep or eat, because of that unforgivable affront to her white person.

Always Agrippa, conscious of the hostility of the white women, would have the lorry key in his hand and claim that he, being Mlambo's son, and having Swazi royal blood in his veins, an expert at his 'work', could never be sacked. He would keep his job. For is it not true that human beings the whole world over will always respect a hardworking man?

I remembered how Mr. Bloch, driven by anger and disgust, would ring the employment agency to send him a reliable driver, and would actually arrange for the new one to come and report for work the next day. When the driver did report, and the moment of final decision came, the boss would find all sorts of excuses to put off the decisive signing of the new employee's pass-book. Then, obviously in a conflict, the boss would again ask the 'new' one to come tomorrow, 'so that the old driver can finish up his work' (whatever that meant). And that would be that.

Why did the boss behave like that, I wondered. Was it really the effect of Jonas' drugs? Or was it the repossessions?

Like most of us, Mr. Bloch was really rather conservative. It is typical of the Jews, my mother had once told me, that when you have worked for them faithfully for a long time, and they are used to you, then they will cling to you like a baby to its mother. They are always chary of taking new servants. I was inclined to believe what my mother had told me. Here was a man who was aware that he was losing a lot of money because of an irresponsible driver but who just could not discharge him.

Yet Agrippa could hardly be considered a faithful worker. What then? Could it be the repossessions – the bringing back of the goods from bad customers to lie in the store? Did the fact that his goods were back in his store-rooms give the boss so much satisfaction that even if Agrippa brought them back in a deplorable state, infested with vermin of every description, he was contented? Repossessing the goods was sometimes an incentive for the customers to pay up the arrears and get the goods back, yes. But then, in the process of delivering, getting them back and redelivering them, the goods were damaged by the grudging lorry-boys who claimed that they were being made to sweat and work hard for nothing. When their persistent begging for more money went unheeded, they were left with no way of negotiating for better wages. Was it surprising that they took out their frustration on the boss's goods? 'He does not pay us,' they would say, cursing and throwing the furniture on or off the lorries.

Indeed, the furniture would be re-delivered to the customers in such a state that they would not mind whether it were repossessed again. They could always go and place another deposit at a better shop where their goods were handled with greater care. And when repossessed goods did lie in the store in pieces, they would cost the boss more money to be re-conditioned so that they could be sold as secondhand goods. In the whole unbusinesslike retrogression caused by the same load of goods continually in transit either from vendor to purchaser or *vice versa,* the only one who stood to gain was the lorry driver because he insisted on being paid for every possession.

'I am definitely dismissing him,' the boss muttered. 'He has had his chips, I'm finished with him. I'm going to take my keys and kick him out!'

Mrs. Kuhn and Mrs. Stein exchanged a sceptical smile, looking at each other and shaking their heads.

There were urgent deliveries to be made. Besides, in the meantime, Ponty had rang from the other shop in town. He had been paid a big cash deposit on a good sale of suites for dining-room, bedroom and sitting-room by a Coloured family in Alexandra township. A trade-in also had to be picked up on that day, otherwise there was the risk of the customers deciding to go and buy elsewhere. Customers can be very impatient when they have paid a cash deposit. They expect prompt service. Ponty had rung again, presumably reminding the boss of the big sale. The boss was in a dilemma. Only Agrippa could penetrate the notorious, gangster-dominated township where strangers walked the streets in fear.

After consulting Jonas, Agrippa went and stood on the other side of the steel rails over the counter, looking at the boss and chewing his 'stick'.

'Don't hang round me, Agrippa!' roared the boss. 'Go and get your boys and collect this trade-in from Alexandra township today!'

'I want petrol, baas.'

'I suppose you drank all my petrol in the four days you were off!'

Agrippa smiled, throwing his head back, boastfully. He had done it again. He said, 'Please, baas, don't waste my time. Alexander is rough. I mustn't be there late at night.'

'Oh, give him a petrol slip, please, Mrs. Stein.'

Agrippa triumphantly took the slip and followed the boss down the passage towards the door.

'What did I tell you, Mrs. Kuhn?' asked the disappointed Mrs. Stein.

In the end I myself was inadvertently responsible for Agrippa's getting the sack. If I had known that for those customers whose cards had been marked FOR REPOSSESSION – PERSONAL SUMMONS ISSUED no more letters are sent, I would not have sent a letter of 'final warning' and the customer would have continued paying to Agrippa, knowing that the driver was keeping the goods safe for the customer. Otherwise, furniture dealers being what they are, the goods would have been repossessed long ago. So for more than a year the customer continued to pay the driver and the driver gave some convincing reason to the credit control manageress. Agrippa would have got away with it. But I was surprised that there had been no response by the customer, and had written the letter. When the customer received the 'final warning' he immediately sent his wife to the shop to find out what such a threatening letter meant. I had inadvertently plunged Agrippa into a trap from which he could not escape.

I was called upon to act as interpreter. Agrippa was pleading with me on the one hand not to interpret correctly, and the customer's wife was furiously threatening Agrippa on the other. They were both speaking in Zulu and I had to explain to the boss what they were both saying. Agrippa kept begging the woman not to press the case, that he would pay all the money back but she was adamant. I was saying such things as the woman was suffering from loss of memory and could not remember when she had last paid. But Mrs. Stein guessed from the woman's gesticulations that what I said was not true. She telephoned the place where the customer worked and asked to speak to him. The truth was uncovered and Agrippa was discharged.

So now Agrippa was working for another firm. Like everybody else, he had his good qualities. Mr. Bloch had been complaining that there were now no repossessions to speak of at all. In all his three shops, there were long lists of pending repossessions.

Daniel, the new lorry driver, was not like Agrippa. He said to me once, 'Mr. Bloch is always grumbling to me about the repossessions and I advised him to go and get Agrippa back. Agrippa is just the right man for him. I don't want to take goods back from the customers. I am not a vulture. I don't go about eating people's strength. I can only go to their homes and speak to these people, make them see that it is important that they should pay. Besides, I can't work until twelve o'clock at night in a place like Soweto. Supper is at six o'clock at my house and my wife expects me to be home by then. Agrippa does not care for his wife and children. All he cares about is getting enough money to drink.'

Later that month, nearly eight weeks after Agrippa had been

discharged, Adam slouched in complete with his Churchill hat pulled low over his head, the broad brim resting on his eyebrows, and his knobkerrie in his hand. He was three hours late. He had met Daniel in the location where he lived and the driver had offered him a lift in the lorry. Daniel had been seeing some of the 'personal summonses' customers. On their way coming to town, the lorry had stopped. He said to me, 'You know, Dan is stuck in Industria with that rorry. Baas said Agrippa was cheating with the petrol and chased him away. But that's not rorry, that's rubbish!'

'What's that, Adam?' The boss had overheard Adam's remark.

'Dat rorry for Dan, baas. He stuck in Industria and I get rift in, baas. Dan ter' me he do reven garrans for forte-two maeres, dat rorry, baas.'

'Daniel told you the lorry had eleven gallons of petrol in only forty-two miles?'

'Yes, baas.'

When Daniel ultimately arrived at the shop, Lennie, the white mechanic, was sent to go out with him and check the petrol consumption of the vehicle. It did exactly six miles to a gallon!

The boss came in rushing with a piece of paper in his hand on which he had written some figures after checking the mileage of the truck himself. He complained saying, 'That thing is eating petrol like hell. It's a waste of time!'

This discovery softened Mr. Bloch's heart towards Agrippa. Perhaps he was not such a cheat after all.

Ignoring the discouraging comments from Mrs. Stein and Mrs. Kuhn, he called Agrippa back. Mrs. Kuhn said, 'What's the use? He'll only start doing the same thing again. He'll flatter you for a while to begin with, but he'll start his nonsense again. He's just as sly as all of them.' And Mrs. Stein advised, 'I would never take a boy or a girl back if I were you. They always think you can't do without them, then they try to boss you around.'

But things had been going badly at Metropolitan Radio. Comparatively less money was coming in from customers who feared that their goods would be repossessed than before. There were also very few goods brought back. So the boss overlooked the comments by his female staff and informed Agrippa that he would like him to return to Metropolitan Radio. Of course the lorry-driver was only too happy to be back. He left the other firm without giving notice. He told everybody happily, 'I am back home!'

When Agrippa was back and was doing his work well, everybody felt that everything was neatly in place. The pieces of the jigsaw puzzle fitted perfectly.

For nearly six weeks after his re-engagement, it looked as though Agrippa had changed. He was drinking less and had not stayed away from work in all that time. It was clear that the lorry driver had come with the determination to prove his real worth, to show his true qualities as the number one lorry-driver for Metropolitan Radio. As usual, he was never reluctant to blow his own trumpet.

'You know, my sister,' he said to me, 'I'm the only one who is allowed to do every type of work in this place. I am the number one lorry-driver and repossessor; but I am also allowed to sell goods for which I am paid extra commission. I am also allowed to have my own receipt book and collect money from difficult customers.'

There had been a marked improvement in the response of

bad customers. One incident made the boss confident that he had made the right decision in re-engaging the repentent lorry-driver.

A customer, Darius Bokako, had placed a thirty-five rand cash deposit on a radiogram which he was anxious to have delivered. Although the customer had said that he had no trade references, the boss had been willing to take the risk because the cash deposit had been 'encouraging'. When Agrippa arrived with the radiogram at the address on the H.P. agreement, the owner of the house claimed that Bokako was not actually living there, that he only paid them occasional visits. Agrippa became suspicious and returned the radiogram to the shop.

Later, Bokako, still keen to have the radiogram, came in to pay an additional twenty rands and explained to the boss that although he had no house of his own at any of the locations, he wanted the radiogram and would pay for it regularly. He also gave the boss the assurance that he would keep it at the stated address and not remove it until he had finished paying for it. With the additional money already paid in, the boss was not difficult to convince. Bokako accompanied Agrippa in the lorry and signed for the radiogram on delivery.

Although the white women were still pessimistic, Mr. Bloch complimented Agrippa on his presence of mind in dealing with Darius Bokako's case. He said, 'I forgive you all your sins, Agrippa.'

The boss said that humbly with a bit of pride, like a woman finding momentary reassurance in her struggles with a wayward alcoholic husband. He added, 'It shows that you can think when you like. If only you could stop drinking so much.'

But it was too good to last. One afternoon Agrippa rang from the Moroka Police Station to say that he had gone to report the loss of his receipt book, which he claimed had disappeared from the seat of his lorry.

'That's nonsense,' snapped Mrs. Kuhn. 'There's no truth in that at all. He must have used up all the money he had collected at the shebeens and now he's scared to come and tell you, Larry. He's a liar. I told you so!'

And Mrs. Stein also took it as a vindication of what she had observed when Mr. Bloch had ignored them and re-instated Agrippa. She remarked, 'You shouldn't have taken him back, Mr. Bloch. Now he knows he's got you where he wants you. He knows you can't do without him; so he takes advantage.'

Misfortune must have been stalking poor Agrippa. The boss's confidence was shaken, and he began to check up on Agrippa. When he found that there apparently had been some misappropriation of trade-in stoves, Mr. Bloch returned from the store in a very bad temper. He said, 'No wonder he has been working so well! He has been selling my stoves!'

When Agrippa reported to work the following day, without his receipt book, Mr. Bloch quickly demanded his pass and signed him off. He enumerated all his sins since he was re-engaged and summed it up by saying, 'Since you came back, you have cost me one hundred and fifty rands, maybe more. Who knows how many more complaints will come dogging your footsteps?'

None of the commission due to him was paid. It would all go towards making good all the money he owed the firm, the boss said. He looked at the piece of paper calmly on which he had written the record of Agrippa's 'crimes', and read them all out loudly once again. The last 'sin' had been the last straw, and Agrippa had finally had his last chance of all.

'Look at those things lying there. I can't be bothered even

to ask you why all those things are there,' the boss said, pointing at a collection of articles on a table next to me. They were a portable radio, glasses, cups and saucers – all broken. They had been brought in by a customer the previous day after her kitchen scheme had been repossessed by Agrippa and his lorryboys. They had arrived at her house dead drunk on Sunday afternoon. Only her children were at home. So, without hesitation, the boys got to work removing all the contents out of the drawers and cupboards of the dresser and throwing them on the floor. The children, scared and trembling, looked on with horror as the radio and crockery were thrown about and broken.

Mr. Bloch pointed at the mess on the floor and said, 'See, I will have to get that portable repaired and I'll have to pay back all those broken articles. I don't want to see you again, *never*!'

The final kick had come at last and in the presence of both the black and white members of the staff.

Mr. Bloch had summoned enough courage to do it alone. He didn't even need the moral support he usually received from the good white ladies. He acted independently.

But the labourers were quite certain that Agrippa would never have been dismissed if he had kept his payments to Jonas – the medicine-man – up to date. For a long time he had been in arrears and Jonas warned him that he would lose his job. When he went into the kitchen to get the 'protection stick' to chew before he uttered a word to the boss, Jonas ignored him. He had therefore had nothing to ward off the 'evil spirits' which had gained entrance into the boss.

20

The mechanic walks out

LENNIE, THE white mechanic, wanted to use the telephone on my desk. As he reached for the receiver, he mumbled something which I could not catch.

'Did you say something?' I asked.

'Yes. I am saying on Monday, you will have to look for another mechanic,' Lennie said, in a whisper. 'I'm leaving.'

'Why?'

'Oh man, I'm sick of this place. There's no need for me to stay now that I've finished my contract. I am a qualified radio mechanic and I can start my own business or work at a better place. Repairs come in and when you want spares, he tells you to wait, that you want to waste money and then the sets lie up there undone. Then when the customers come for them, he wants to know why they are not ready. He tells me I'm stupid and moans in front of the customers. And the number of times he has used me as a driver! Sometimes I have to leave sets lying on my table unassembled for days just driving him around, and he thinks nothing of the time he makes me waste. He makes me do work he does not pay me for. I could easily get him into trouble if I wanted to. I know the law, and I know what I am entitled to.

'No, on Friday, tomorrow, when I walk out at five-thirty, the tool-box will be in my hand, and I won't come and work here again … I'm sick and tired of it!' Lennie finished in disgust, still holding the receiver in his hand and not dialling a number.

'Have you given in your notice?'

'No. Why should I?'

'Surely you can't just walk out like that?'

'Why not? He can't do anything to me; he can go to hell!'

I was taken aback when Lennie told me of his intentions – surprised that he spoke to me at all. Apart from the occasions when he would ask, 'Muriel, can you lend me twenty cents, I'll give it back tomorrow,' Lennie hardly ever spoke to us. In fact I could count the times when he did.

The first time was when he was taking me in the van to the pass office for registration. On the way, he asked me, 'Muriel, tell me, what are you?'

'What do you mean, what am I?'

'Are you a teacher or something?'

'No. I'm not a teacher.'

'What are you then?'

'I am just myself – just a person. Why do you ask?'

And that was where it ended. He said no more until the next occasion.

It was just after the late Robert Kennedy had visited the Republic. I had borrowed the pamphlet printed during his visit and was reading it, when Lennie stopped by my desk and asked me, 'Why are you reading that? Are you a Communist?'

'What do you mean, a Communist?' I asked him.

But again, he said no more.

Another time he asked me to take over the account he had of a set of encyclopaedias, which I refused because they were too expensive for me.

The last time was when he happened to notice a group of African mine-workers who had just walked into the shop. They were being served by Adam, and I had paid them no attention, until Lennie called me, 'Muriel, do you see that green cap that boy is wearing?'

I looked up and saw the cap, which was made of green floral material with flaps to cover the ears and a rather lengthy brim. To me, it was nothing extraordinary. It looked just like any other cap except that it was rather colourful to be worn by a man. I looked at the mechanic enquiringly. He said, 'Do you know what that cap is? Do you know where it comes from?'

I shook my head, wondering why he should expect me to know about men's headgear. I said, 'Why do you ask?'

He called to the man wearing it by whistling to him. When the man doubtfully left the group and walked nearer, Lennie said, 'Ask him. Just ask him where he got that cap from. You'll hear.'

I pointed to the cap on the man's head and asked him in Fanagalo where he had bought it. He removed the cap from his head, looked at it, and said, 'This? I did not buy it.'

'Where did you get it then?' I asked.

'Angola,' the man answered.

Lennie smiled and said, 'You see, I knew! It's the cap used by the terrorists in Angola and Mozambique.'

On Friday afternoon, Lennie brought a number of comics and magazines and deposited them on my desk, saying, 'Here, Muriel, you can have these – I don't need them any more.'

'Thanks,' I said mechanically. Only then did I remember what he had said the previous day. He must be clearing his working bench, I realised, so he must have been serious.

At five twenty-seven, Lennie descended the stairs. In his hand he was carrying his tool-box as he had said. The boss was already occupying his usual position next to the till and facing the door. As Lennie turned at the bend of the passage, Mr. Bloch asked, looking at the tool-box in Lennie's hand, 'What are you carrying in that box, Lennie?'

'It's my tool-box,' Lennie said, walking down the passage without looking back.

The boss shouted after him, 'Why are you taking it with you?'

'Because it's mine!' Lennie shouted back as he went out through the front doors. Mrs. Stein who was removing her jacket from the 'Whites Only' coat-hanger, looked at Mr. Bloch and said, 'You'll never see him again, Mr. Bloch. He told me ...'

Before she could say anything more, Mr. Bloch interrupted her, 'I don't care! I don't want to see him; he can go! He is not much of a mechanic anyway. I'm only sorry that I did not look to see what he's got in that tool-box of his. I don't want him. He's too stupid. Even Willy, the Coloured at the store, is better than him!'

I thought I knew why Lennie had decided to walk out.

We were all dissatisfied, all trying to get the best out of life, but we were struggling on different battlefields. For the whites, the struggle was that of human beings trying to better themselves. For the blacks it was that of the underdogs, voiceless and down-trodden. In addition to the difficult task of making a living, we still had to labour under the effects of a rigid apartheid system supported by our own colleagues. Yet we had the same problems. We were all under the thumb of a demanding boss, who was unyielding in many ways, giving little consideration to the fact that we had private lives of our own, homes and dependants to look after.

Office workers, mechanics, technicians, we were all more or less engaged in the same tasks at the same time. The colour of our skins did not come into it – there was work to be done, and the boss had equal confidence in all of us. When there was an error in the office records, he did not care what colour the hand was that made the error, only whose handwriting it was. When a radio or motor was damaged in the workshop, it did not matter if the mechanic responsible was white or black.

The crux of the matter was that the white workers did not want to acknowledge their commonness with their black colleagues. As long as the system granted them certain privileges that the other racial groups did not enjoy, then they were contented. If they were treated the same, they grew resentful.

21

'What's happening to us?'

ONE MORNING I arrived at the shop and was greeted with stony glances by the white women. I did not blame them. I was three hours late. Mrs. Kuhn said sarcastically, 'Good afternoon, madam!'

Mrs. Stein observed, also sarcastically, with a sardonic smile, 'Honestly, Muriel, what do you think you are now – manageress of Metropolitan Radio or what? Last week it was something about the checking of your residential permit, which took nearly the whole day, then three days after that you had to submit the birth certificates of all your children to that same office, which took half the day, then on Monday this week you had to go and pay your rent! What is it this time?'

By the time Mrs. Stein had finished enumerating the string of excuses, they sounded quite unreal and absurd – like a tissue of deliberate lies. Who can believe that such things can happen? Mrs. Stein went on, 'Mr. Bloch was waiting impatiently for you to come because we had two customers who wanted to sign H.P.s. He's really furious you know …'

I interrupted, 'I am sure Mr. Bloch is not as irritated as I am. I have notes here to show why I am late.'

I put the sheets of paper on the desk in front of her and went to hang up my coat.

'What's this?' She started reading from the first sheet of paper. '"You are requested to report to Meadowlands Police tomorrow at 8 a.m." What's all this? What's it about?'

'I had to appear at the Security Branch of the Meadowlands Police Station this morning.'

For the first time the women showed interest by looking up at me and listening. Mrs. Stein asked, 'The Security Branch? Are you a spy or what?'

'I had to go and say whether I have any objection to a visit from my sister's daughter during the December holidays. Also that I know her identity and who she is. The security police have called at my place several times, but last night they left that note saying that I must appear. She must have applied for a permit to pay me a visit.'

'Where is she from?'

'From Botswana.'

'Where?'

'Bechuanaland.'

'Why didn't you say so then? What did you call it ... Bo – what?'

'Botswana. It's not called Bechuanaland any more now.'

'Oh. Is that all, you were visited by the security police several times only to say you know who your sister's daughter is? It sounds childish to me. What for, didn't you ask?'

'I was told it's for security reasons. Our security might be threatened by her visit or that of unknown persons, I understand.'

'What do you mean "our security", who's *our*?'

'The security of all of us, everybody in this Republic. That's

193

why I've got to keep Mr. Bloch waiting and everybody else.'

And I thought to myself, to think that my poor little niece is not even aware that she is so important. That her innocent request to pay me a visit can be regarded as a threat to the security of the inhabitants of the great Republic of South Africa.

'There's a girl waiting to sign an H.P., Muriel.'

'Where? That's Anna Gxagxa, an old customer of ours. She has paid up her account. Perhaps she just wants to chat with me a bit.'

'Yes, but now she wants to buy that maroon carpet. She's a good customer – paid up all her balance on that other account, thirty-six rands. Mr. Bloch doesn't want us to lose her. Said she could have the carpet on account without deposit. She can start paying her instalment at the end of next month. He gave her a cash bonus of five rands, that will serve as her deposit.'

I went over to the customer.

'Good morning, Anna.'

'Good morning, my sister. I've been waiting a long time for you.'

'But you haven't been lonely. Adam has been keeping you company. I see you two have been having tea together. So you want that maroon carpet? How much did Mr. Bloch say she can have it for, Adam?'

'Ninety rands. It's not brand new – if it were it would cost a hundred pounds. Anna is very lucky. Mr. Bloch likes her because she is one of our best customers, always pays fast.'

'Anna, you are dressed in maroon from head to toe – everything maroon – and now you want to buy a maroon carpet?'

'Yes, maroon is my favourite colour.'

'And it suits you,' I said.

Joseph, the tall, stout pompous salesman, walked in with unshaven beard. The black and white stubble spread over his ample chin like some weedy vegetation. He looked harassed and slovenly. He was not wearing the dark grey suit and the spotlessly white shirt he customarily wore on such days. The pair of trousers he had on was torn and patched on the seat and greasy on the knees, and he wore no tie. He did not seem to be in good spirits as he normally was and he was spitting more frequently than usual – into the palms of his hands, on the floor, into the waste-paper basket, everywhere.

'Where are the other men, haven't they come in yet?' Joseph asked.

'No, I haven't seen anyone since I arrived. They might have arrived earlier, I don't know.'

Joseph snapped, 'Oh well, they know what to expect. I'm sick of Mr. Bloch, man.' And he spat into the waste-paper basket. 'He only thinks of pleasing those women, not us, and he knows that they are very mean to us. When we speak to customers on the telephone they don't like it. They always cut us off purposely on that switchboard. How are we supposed to work?'

Pointing at Mrs. Stein, he said, 'We bring in orders for goods and she sits down and wastes time deliberately, then these goods are not delivered on time. By the time they are delivered, the customers don't accept them because they can get them elsewhere. There's a lot of competition. He does not seem to realise that. *They* look after the interests of the salesmen – not like here where a woman with skirts gets in your way all the time. These women! Always pretending to be better than everybody else. Why can't he get more of our girls? Afraid they'll put them in the shade? Ag, man, I'm fed up. If this goes on,

I'll double-cross him. I'll take orders elsewhere where they can be dealt with promptly. I like to work hard, but I don't like to be pushed around.'

And Joseph walked out without saying good-bye.

'Maybe he quarrelled with his wife,' Adam said, and Anna and I laughed.

'But this nauseating habit of his annoys me,' Adam complained, frowning.

'That spitting of his! It was worse today!' I agreed.

'Does he always do it?' Anna asked.

'Yes. I think he must be spitting to kill the evil spirits all around him.'

The scooters roared in quick succession onto the pavements. The salesmen walked into the shop carrying briefcases like bigwigs or business consultants. They greeted us one by one as they passed to a secluded spot near the linoleum squares.

Silas came over to us to use the telephone on my desk. He picked up the receiver, and there was a buzz on the switchboard.

'Who's picking up the receiver there, Muriel?' Mrs. Stein asked.

'It's myself, madam,' answered Silas. 'Can I use the line for a moment, please?'

'Don't be long, I am expecting a call from our store-room, there's a customer waiting for a chassis here.'

'Thank you, ma'am.' And Silas said softly to us as he was dialling the number, 'If it had been the other madam, I would not have got the line.'

And I remembered what Joseph had said.

'What is this lady buying, Muriel?' Silas asked when he had finished his call. 'Why did she not get it through us? It's always better to buy your goods through a salesman, my sister, because we can always persuade the boss to arrange suitable terms.'

'What you are trying to do, Silas, take our own shop customers away? You are too late, because she is an old customer of ours. She has finished paying for her dining-room suite, and now she wants a carpet.'

Silas looked disappointed.

Anna said, 'I only hope your boss will deliver my carpet soon. When you have bought something, you want to see it in your house and not in the shop.'

'Where do you live, Dude Village?' Silas asked.

'No, Zola.'

'Oh, I thought you were one of those African "tycoons" who were lucky enough to buy a house.'

'What do you mean lucky? Surely anyone can buy a house if he's got the money, can't he?' Anna asked.

Silas merely smiled.

Anna was obviously disturbed by Silas's remark. She persisted, 'What did you mean about buying a house, my brother?'

'Don't you know that the buying has been stopped, my sister? Those who bought long ago are the only lucky ones.'

'To me it's just nonsense,' I put in. 'What kind of house have you bought if you know that when you die, your wife and children cannot claim it as legal owners, or stay in it as of right? As soon as you go, their right to stay in it also goes and they can be bundled off at any moment!'

'It's better than having no house at all, and paying rent indefinitely. Your wife and children can at least sell it after you are dead,' Silas said.

'And do what, go where? Living in the townships is like living on shifting sands. Every Parliamentary session brings in fresh, more oppressive laws. One month there is hope for some security, the next brings despair. Sometimes I wonder why we bother to buy furniture at all,' said Anna.

'Well, I suppose like people the world over, we want to feel that we possess something. We need something firm to hold on to, even if it is only a piece of wood. It gives life a meaning, just to hurry home and sit and look at the furniture, even if it is ill suited for the brick boxes they build for us,' I said.

'They tell you that you can go to the Bantustans and buy or build any house you feel like building, don't you know?' Silas said, grinning sardonically.

'Who wants to go there and starve to death? There are no factories, no business places, no towns.'

'Besides, these Bantustans could never accommodate all of us. How could the Africans, millions of them, be expected to cramp into that fraction of land (arid land at that), when a handful of whites own all the rest?'

'And the land really belongs to *us*, mind you,' put in Anna.

'The fact is that Africa – from Cape to Cairo – is the black man's country, just as Europe is a white man's country. If black people went and settled at the tip of Europe – Italy or Spain for example – then we could claim that it is Black South Europe, like they call Southern Africa White South Africa. Then we could keep ourselves in power with slogans like "Keep Black South Europe Black".'

We all laughed. Then Silas resumed, 'People are being thrown out of their houses in Johannesburg and told to go back to their original "homes" where their grandfathers or great-grandfathers came from.'

'There are too many of us, and many more are being born every day. Where are all these people going to be housed? They cannot cope with the teeming numbers, so they find all sorts of excuses to drive people away,' I said.

'But some of these people who are told to leave are old. They have spent all their lives here. Where can you go and build a new home when you are already old? The whites even like their cats and dogs better than they like us,' Anna said, speaking sadly. 'Last year I wanted to go to Rustenburg and I was told by my missus that I couldn't go. My husband and children went alone and I had to remain and cook for my employers' dogs and cats because the family were all leaving for Cape Town on holiday. My missus said if I went too the cats and dogs would starve to death. My heart was very sore because it was Easter season and our church had organised a prayer session in Rustenburg.'

'Which is your church?' Adam asked.

'Father McCamel's Church.'

'Was it for Maroon Day?'

'Yes.'

Adam looked at me and smiled. I guessed what he was thinking. In loyalty to the firm, we dared not laugh in case Anna decided to change her mind about the maroon carpet.

Mr. Bloch walked in and the discussion ended. Silas left in a hurry, and I remembered that I still had to account for my lateness in the morning.

'Where were you now, Muriel? The whole morning customers were waiting here, and ...'

The boss would have gone on scolding me, but Mrs. Stein came to my rescue by showing him the notes I had brought with me in the morning. As the boss hastily looked at them I apologised, 'I am very sorry, Mr. Bloch, but I could not help it.'

I looked up Anna's pass number from her old card and

wrote it on the H.P. agreement which I handed over to the boss.

'I see from the other card that your dining-room suite has maroon seats and backs to the chairs,' I said to Anna. 'So your dining-room will be all maroon.'

'Yes, my curtains are maroon, too. I *do* like maroon. I think it is beautiful. It has dignity.'

When Mr. Bloch had assured Anna that her carpet would be delivered that very evening, Anna left happily.

22

One human heart for another

I HAD BEEN elevated to a higher position. I was no longer the least junior because I had someone under me – an assistant.

Of all the many African girls who had come for an interview and a test since we had advertised for an African female clerk/typist, Daisy was the best suited. She had good legible handwriting, and she was fast on the typewriter. I liked her cool yet confident composure. Her marked fluency in both English and Afrikaans made her, besides Mrs. Stein and myself, more bilingual than all the white women who had worked at Metropolitan Radio while I was there. She also spoke many African languages. She is more of a true South African citizen than any of them, I said to myself.

I could hear Daisy complaining about the heat to Adam.

'It is as though someone were slowly pouring hot water down my spine.'

Adam was leaning over the steel cabinets and watching her work. She was continually wiping her lovely face with a saturated handkerchief. The heat seemed to affect Adam less, but he answered sympathetically, 'They have three fans on the other side but they would never give you one. They're selfish. In winter they take all the heaters onto their side and in summer, they let all the fans face towards them.'

From where I was sitting, making journal entries, I could hear the monotonous sound made by Daisy turning the handle of the addressograph machine. Thank God I did not have to address those four thousand statements any more. Daisy had taken over from me the more mechanical tasks and I was thankful. I had to occupy the desk on the 'white' side of the line more frequently and for the greater part of the month because I was doing books and helping the bookkeeper, Mrs. Kuhn.

The white women had come to look upon me not as a danger but as a co-worker. Even Mrs. Stein, the diehard Afrikaner, who for months would never utter my name, had grown to like me. No, I think tolerate is a better word for it. She would sometimes even engage in casual conversation with me, especially when Mrs. Kuhn was not present. She passed many household hints to me. Like most Afrikaner women, she was an excellent housewife and a good mother. She would tell me a lot about her own children, and would divulge some of her concern and fears for them. Occasionally, she brought photographs of her children to show us.

Quite often, on Monday mornings, Mrs. Stein would bring in samples of dishes she had prepared for her family during the week-end, neatly wrapped in spotlessly white cloths, for all of us to taste. Her embroidery, knitting, crocheting and smocking were all perfect.

As for Mrs. Kuhn, I had now almost forgiven her all her past atrocities against me. She was a great little lady, always hardworking, and she too was a devoted mother. She seemed so fragile, she used to induce within me the desire to protect her. I used to offer to carry the heavy typewriters for her to wherever she wanted them when the 'boys' were not in the shop.

Fate had not been kind to her. She had lost her beautiful talented daughter, at the height of her career as a dancer, in a fatal car accident. Why should such tragedies occur? I used to ask myself whenever I looked at her and thought of her beloved Molly, who had (to quote from Trollope) 'a dignity of demeanour devoid of all stiffness or pride'. It was now over a year since she had met her death. I had thought that her mother would never recover from it, never be able to smile again. But because God is great and can heal all wounds, Mrs. Kuhn could still come to work and laugh as she always did.

When Mrs. Kuhn first came back to work after nearly a month's absence, Adam was the first to offer condolences on behalf of the black workers at Metropolitan Radio. Adam had known Molly since she was a child and her tragic death had obviously touched him. He began softly, looking down at her bereaved mother, 'I very sorry, missus …' but Mrs. Kuhn snapped bitterly, 'You ought to rejoice. It was your people who did it!' To me the sad incident demonstrated how inextricably the lives of whites and non-whites are interwoven.

Then there was Mrs. Singham, the latest of the many cashiers we had already had, and the one who held that position longest. She was English-speaking and like Mrs. Kuhn could speak almost no Afrikaans at all, a factor I could never understand. The whites of the Republic of South Africa can be so segregated in the imaginary oneness. Mrs. Singham was very kind and humane. She enjoyed reading books and used to discuss them with me. She also enjoyed listening to music. We used to exchange long-playing records and books.

Sitting with these women, I was thinking of Daisy. Why should she sit sweltering behind the steel cabinets on the other side, less than six feet away from us, while we were cool and comfortable? Why should I be the only one feeling uneasy? Or was I the only one? Maybe if one of them had felt like helping Daisy, she was afraid of being considered *kaffir-boetie** as much as I feared being accused of being an agitator. I dared not plead on her behalf even in my newly-acquired status as senior helper.

These people were not inhuman nor were they downright cruel, as I used to brand them all. I had learned that they could be kind and gentle. If only this fear of us could be removed somehow. I had painfully learned that, for the best results, one must coax them slowly and gradually. I had learned that one must not be too abrupt, too precipitate, and too ready to condemn. I had almost succeeded in removing a great deal of the suspicion. For example, when one of them dropped something, I quickly picked it up and handed it to her. I even offered to go to the shops or chemist or some of the nearby places when all the 'boys' were busy loading. I had taken upon my shoulders the difficult task of teaching them that the black African is no *gogga*† but a human being.

Mr. Bloch had employed Daisy because he knew that it would cost him more – possibly three or four times more – to employ a white woman to assist Mrs. Kuhn. He naturally preferred to use me instead.

The heat was unbearable for Daisy. No wonder she went on looking for another job in town where there were better working conditions, and when she got it, she left without giving notice at the end of that very month. Not all of us have the submissive forbearance of a lamb. She never even bade me good-

---

* derogatory term to describe a white person who associates with or speaks up for the Africans, the so-called 'kaffirs'. (Afrikaans)
† something that provokes fear in the beholder; something ugly.

bye. Possibly she thought I was a traitor. My hard-earned state of seniority was short-lived. It had lasted exactly thirty days.

'Just lend me that pen of yours, Muriel, please,' Mrs. Stein asked.

She was standing at the switchboard holding the receiver with one hand and reaching out to me with the other. She was speaking to a European lady, presumably an employer of one of our African customers. I used to enjoy listening to her speak on the telephone, so I stopped listening to Adam and Daisy and listened to Mrs. Stein instead. She was speaking in Afrikaans. Her voice, normally harsh, offensive and guttural when speaking to Africans, was transformed into smooth beautiful tones. The word *Mevrouw** was lavishly used. It punctuated almost every sentence or phrase. It struck me that this Afrikaans could be a beautiful language after all.

Mrs. Stein replaced the receiver and clicked her tongue.

'I get so fed up when they speak like that about their servants. Her girl must have received a letter and she wants us to wait until doomsday for her payment. She admits that the girl has not paid for nearly nine months but she still expects us to give her a chance.'

Mrs. Kuhn was annoyed. 'You should have asked her how much she pays that girl per month if she is so kind. For all I know she never pays her her full salary and perhaps that's why she can't pay up. If she feels so sorry for the girl why doesn't she pay off the radio for her?'

'I suppose she can't take the risk, but she expects *us* to take it. Give her the radio for nothing. She could pay it off and take it out of her salary every month. She wants to know why we let

---

* Mrs. (Afrikaans)

them take goods worth so much when we know they can't afford it. How are we supposed to know? I asked her whether she was prepared to sign security for her and she said she would have to speak to her husband! How do you like that, Mrs. Kuhn?'

'And I bet that's the last time you hear from her, Mrs. Stein. You should have told her that we are sending someone to repossess the radio immediately, and that even if we do, her girl must still pay the balance. *That* would give her something to think about.'

Just then the tea-boy passed and Mrs. Stein called him.

'Jonas, go and buy me the newspapers. Get me the *Transvaler* and the *Star*.'

Mrs. Singham looked up. 'Did you read last night's paper? The heart transplant was a success.'

The other two said they had seen it.

Mrs. Singham asked, 'But they put a Coloured's heart into a white man. How can they do that when they believe in apartheid?'

That sparked off one of the most heated arguments I have ever heard. I kept quiet and listened.

Mrs. Stein immediately took up the remark as if it were a personal challenge. 'Well, you see, Mrs. Singham, the heart is merely a muscle. It merely pumps the blood.'

I could not resist asking, 'Surely the Coloured's heart was not cleaned out or sterilised first to make sure that none of his blood would be introduced into the white man's veins?'

Mrs. Singham said, 'It couldn't have been altogether drained of the Coloured's blood. And possibly the Coloured's blood was of the same group as that of the white man so that his system would not reject it.'

'In any case,' I said more firmly, 'blood is blood and the

four main human blood groups are found in every racial group. There is no such thing as white blood or non-white blood.'

Mrs. Singham agreed. 'The whole thing is ridiculous.'

'Mind you, we've also had whites as donors for Bantus and Coloureds,' Mrs. Stein said, looking first at Mrs. Singham and then at me. 'What about that kidney transplant we were reading about the other day, Mrs. Kuhn?'

'Yes, Mrs. Stein, but that's for a kidney and not the heart. I can understand about the kidney, but the heart!'

'To me your heart is your soul,' Mrs. Singham said, emphasising the last word.

'How South Africa's enemies will howl,' Mrs. Kuhn said, shaking her head sadly.

'Yes, they'll say these whites here are hypocrites,' I added, 'that when they are faced with death and are in fear, they shed all their pride.'

'It just goes to show that all people are the same,' said Mrs. Singham.

Mrs. Stein was not disposed to agree. 'The critics overseas are ill-informed about the true situation. They only receive false information. South Africa is a most peaceful country. People are free to go where they like, and say what they feel, I mean …'

She went on to insist that all racial groups were happy and living with each other in harmony, how for nearly a decade now there had not been any uprisings or strikes unlike other countries such as America where there were killings and riots. I listened, trying very hard to be patient. I could not understand how anyone in full control of his or her faculties could claim that South Africa was a peaceful country, that all its people were happy.

But Mrs. Kuhn was looking at Mrs. Stein nodding her head in approval to all that she was saying. She smiled and looked at me.

'Yes, Muriel, they're free to visit each other at any time.'

I replied, 'What you say about people being free to move and free to say what they like is perhaps true of the whites but not of the blacks. When I want to visit a relation of mine in another location, I must first obtain permission from the superintendent of that location. Otherwise if the police find me there and discover that I do not live there, I can be arrested. As an African, I can be asked to produce my pass at any time and anywhere and I can be searched; also my house can be searched at any time of the day or night. We are *not* free to move. Thousands are arrested every month for offences involving movement. How many times have we sent someone out to the police stations to pay a fine and plead for the release of our own black workers here? And about speech – the blacks are not free to say what they feel. How can they? They may not hold political meetings. All political organisations have been banned. The blacks are voiceless.'

Mrs. Stein scoffed, 'What do you mean, voiceless?'

'They have no vote. They may not choose anyone to represent them in a parliament which makes laws for them.'

'But they can write in their papers how they feel, I know they do not have M.P.s here but they are given their own areas where they can say what they like and have their own cabinet ministers.'

Mrs. Stein spoke proudly and loudly. She might have been standing on Mount Everest and telling the world, so proud she seemed to be. She was speaking as if that was something unique, an offer the Africans should be thankful for.

Mrs. Kuhn joined in.

'Yes, Muriel, look at the Transkei.'

I tried very hard to remain calm. 'Oh, you mean the

Bantustans. But there are more Africans in the cities, living with the whites, than there are in the Bantustans. Most of the voters for representatives to the Transkeian parliament are the people who stay in the towns with the whites. Some of them stay in the compounds and hostels, some are in the locations and they have their homes here. Surely people should be given rights where they are? Most of the voters whose great-grandfathers originally came from the Transkei were born and bred here in the towns. They have never been to these Bantustans and they do not know them. The Bantustans are underdeveloped and backward. Ever since the white man first came to this land, the labour of the Africans and the other non-white groups has been used to develop the towns and the cities. These Bantustans are the poorest areas that able-bodied men and women are only happy to flee from. In any case, it is unlikely that the Africans will ever all migrate to the Bantustans because their labour is needed by the whites in the towns.

'What is the point of giving people rights in far-off places where they have never lived – places they know nothing about? How can I vote for anybody to represent me in a place where I have never lived and don't want ever to live?'

They seemed amazed. It was as if I was saying things they had never heard before. Mrs. Stein made an effort to reply.

'Anyway, Muriel, the Bantus here are better off than those in the other African countries.'

Maybe she said it in good faith. But I had an answer for her.

'Would you be willing to change places with me, Mrs. Stein, go and live in my house and let me live in yours?'

'Well, no,' she admitted.

'Why not, Mrs. Stein?' I asked politely. 'Is it because what is good enough for me is not good enough for you?'

She replied, 'For one thing, our standard of living is not the same.'

'Why?' I asked. Mrs. Stein was reluctant to answer. It was Mrs. Singham who replied.

'Surely, Muriel, you wouldn't expect a native girl from the farms to be paid the same as yourself, would you?'

'Why not?' I asked. 'If we do the same work at the same place it is only logical that we should earn the same, isn't it? Mrs. Singham, do you really believe that the blacks are happy, that they are satisfied with their low standard of living, that they don't mind going hungry when others are rich and well-fed?'

Instead of replying, she asked another question.

'But Muriel, what do you think would happen if the Europeans left and went back to Europe? The black people would massacre one another, wouldn't they?'

Mrs. Kuhn, who had been quiet for some time, came to life.

'Yes. Look at what happened in the Congo!'

It was always raised as an example of the inability of the Africans to govern themselves. I sighed.

'Why did the Belgians keep all doors closed to the Africans for all those years until the eleventh hour? Why did they not train the Africans in local administration first and give them responsible positions gradually, why did they wait until the people *demanded* rights? If they had been given adequate education and prepared, they would have been able to take over without disastrous results.'

Mrs. Stein snapped in quickly, 'Everybody would want to be boss!'

'But if you had some good education, you would be able to judge better. You would be aware that your knowledge was inadequate. When you are ignorant, you still think you know. But once you start to learn, you realise that you must go on learning; you stop assuming that you know. Nobody is born with the knowledge of how to govern. The whites who legislate for others have also had to learn, haven't they?'

For about a minute, there was an uneasy quiet. Then Mrs. Kuhn broke the silence.

'The whole thing is not right. They should have transplanted a white person's heart into that patient, not a Coloured's heart.'

Mrs. Singham asked thoughtfully, 'What would you say is the racial group of a white person in whom a non-white's organs have been transplanted?'

Nobody answered. Everybody went quiet. My thoughts went drifting along the same line of 'whiteness' and 'non-whiteness' ...

How could a body be said to be purely white, with a Coloured heart? Surely this would make the recipient non-white ... And if the law could make it legal for donors and recipients to exchange organs freely, irrespective of colour, and hence change white recipients into non-white people, then would the law not be guilty of committing an immoral act, according to itself?

My mind went on pondering the absurdities and contradictions in this whole matter. It should have been discussed, I said to myself. After all, they sit in parliament and discuss whether a white hand may or may not shake a non-white one!

23

I quit

IT WAS A typical early January morning. There were no customers coming into the shop. No wonder the boss chose this post-Christmas period for leaving Metropolitan Radio behind and going away on holiday.

Adam sat facing the door at his post, well out of sight of the white women and Ricky, the store-manager. Adam was facing the door but from where I was, I could see that he was dozing. He, too, was tired like the rest of us. Why is there no public holiday after New Year's Day? There should be one really, like there is Boxing Day after Christmas Day.

I sat looking at the new calendar. It was only the second day in January and I was already counting the infinite number of days we would be waiting to get my next salary. The month stood there unashamedly long and merciless. After the Christmas and New Year's Day expenses, there were still the children's uniforms, school fees, bus and train fares, food and so on. Even if I were to spend the maximum amount of fifty cents per day (if you can imagine such a possibility), I could still not manage with what was left of my husband's salary and mine combined. How on earth was I to make ends meet?

I was still speculating, looking at the calendar when Jonas threw a card in front of me. I looked at it. What was written as its heading was like an act of derision. It bore the greeting: HAPPY MORNING!

Just think of that – Happy Morning, of all mornings, the second day of January – the 'longest' month in the whole calendar!

Yet little did I realise how significant those words on that card, which Jonas unconcernedly deposited on the desk before me, would be to me. Looking at it, I never suspected that that day would not only be different from all the other days I had spent at Metropolitan Radio but that it would also be decisive.

I was feeling particularly despondent that morning. Yet I was about to cast a bombshell. And what precipitated it came through Little William, of all people.

Ever since I had been persuaded to give up the idea of leaving, I had been drifting along, not quite resigned to the fact. Although I had accepted the offer and had decided to stay on, I knew in my heart that sooner or later, I would have to go. It was only a matter of time before that feeling or restlessness would come back again.

None of my co-workers on the other side of the steel bars seemed to be plagued by the anxiety of where their next meal would come from. On the contrary, they were speaking of the joys of living, of going away or coming back from holiday. Mrs. Stein was relating how much she had enjoyed her last holiday on the South coast – in fact the tan on her neck, bare arms and shoulders was still slightly visible. Mrs. Kuhn, on the other hand, was speaking of how she was envying the boss and his wife, who by then were well on their way to a memorable holiday, away from it all.

Only the ever-faithful, so-called Little William could be working on the second day in January, a day on which no other salesman would even think of coming to the shop, let alone working. He walked in, smiling as usual, carrying in one hand a portogram, and in the other, two portable radios.

'Happy, happy, happy, everybody!' William said, smiling and looking round at Ricky and the white women on the other side. Nobody seemed to take any notice of him, nor did any of them respond to his well-wishing.

Undeterred, he put the radios on the floor next to me and went to fetch the service book from the counter. After he had finished writing out cards for the radios, he came smiling towards me.

'Happy New Year, my sister, I have here a present for you which I know will make you very happy.'

'Same to you, William. What present is it?'

William glanced around like a thief and asked me, 'Where's Adam? I must be sure that nobody hears what we are going to say. It's lucky that those whites are busy yapping.'

'Adam is behind the linos. What's all the mystery about?'

'There's someone who wants to steal you from Metropolitan. He says he'll offer you forty, even fifty, pounds a month if you come and work for him. I know that the boss wouldn't want to lose you. But then, if another employer offers you more money, you can't refuse, can you? After all, we all have to live.'

I did not know what to say. I just looked at him and said nothing.

'Muriel, you don't seem to understand. I would jump sky-high if I had such luck. I am telling you that this European at this place wants to offer you a lot of money – he wants to employ you as a general office clerk at his garage. Can't you see what that means?'

I took the card from William and looked at it. It was the second card I had been given that morning. This one brought with it prospects of hope. It was too good to be true.

'Who is he? How does he know that I work here? And what does he know about the kind of work I do?'

'This white man has been to this place several times to collect his cheque. He thinks you are quite capable of doing any type of work in his office. He also knows that the boss is a stingy man and that you might be underpaid.'

'But who is he?'

'There's his name on the card. We do all our scooter repairs at his garage. He said that I must give you the card and ask you to telephone him at any time when you have the chance.'

At tea-time I went over to Gant's tea-room and dialled the number on the card. A jarring, loud male voice answered. He spoke with an unmistakably foreign accent.

'Continental Scooter Repairs, good morning.'

'Is that Mr. Saladino?'

'No. Would you like to speak to him? He's in the workshop.'

'Yes, please.'

'All right. Just hang on.'

I waited. After a few seconds, Mr. Saladino came to the phone.

'Hallo! Who's speaking?'

'It's Muriel, from Metropolitan ... I ...'

'Oh yes, Muriel. I told William to tell you to ring me. Can you come and work for me?'

'Yes,' I said, suddenly making up my mind. 'When do you want me to start?'

'Now, if you like. You see, my brother here has been doing the office work, and now he has to go home to Italy in two weeks' time. Now I'll have to get someone. When can you come over? Can you come early tomorrow morning and see where we are and what we have to do so that you can start as soon as possible?'

'Yes. But I'm still employed by Metropolitan. And I'll have to give two weeks' notice before I can leave. It's the law.'

'Yes, I know, but you can come in every morning for an hour so that my brother can show you the work.'

I remembered Continental Scooter Repairs. They were situated in Doornfontein. I also remembered how Mrs. Kuhn had once accused them on the telephone of being money-grabbers. On one occasion, after a heated conversation with one of the staff there, she said, 'These immigrants would steal the gold out of your teeth!'

Time and again, she questioned them about the exorbitant sums of money they charged for repairs. Whenever she made out cheques at the end of the month, I would hear her complaining that they were as poor as church mice when they came to the Republic, but became rich overnight.

It looked as if I had got a good job. I agreed to go to Doornfontein every morning for an hour before I started work at Metropolitan. The card Jonas had put on the desk before me had brought with it a pleasant surprise.

Before Christmas Mr. Bloch had taken on some temporary help in the form of a Mrs. Ludorf, who had stayed on although the rush was over. Now she came and sat next to me, a good distance away from Mrs. Singham and Mrs. Stein. I realised then that word that I had resigned and given a month's notice had got round. When she first came, she used to embarrass me, but now she had come to be 'friendly' towards me in a propitiating sort of way. She was always being reminded of her nanny at her house, and she would relate to the other white women some incident about the nanny's ignorance and stupidity. Or she would pass some apparently 'innocent' remark about my vital statistics and about the mealie-pap diet we 'natives' were in the habit of devouring in great quantities.

One day I told her frankly to keep her remarks to herself. Ever since she had gone out of her way to recapture my goodwill. She gossiped rather too frankly about all the other whites.

I knew what was coming when she moved her chair nearer to me and started speaking softly.

'So you want to leave Metropolitan, I believe?'

'Yes.'

'You've got yourself a good job. Where is it?'

'Doornfontein.'

'But I don't believe Mr. Bloch will let you go when he comes back from holiday. I think he'll bargain with you – make offers, you know.'

'I don't think he will. I do not expect him to do so.'

'Why not?'

'Mrs. Singham told me that if he does, she'll ask for far more.'

'Did she really say that?'

'Yes, she did, and point blank. Mrs. Singham is always very frank with me.'

'Jealous! And she hasn't even got what you've got. I believe you've been to university?'

'Where did you hear that from?'

'I just know. She hasn't got half the education you have; can't even type, but she's already getting nearly three times what you get. How much did your boss give you for Christmas bonus?'

'Nothing. But he gave me a travelling rug worth about eight rands.'

'What, a lousy blanket, after all these years? That's a shame! And you know what he gave them?'

I shook my head slowly. 'I don't want to know. Anyway, I need the money, he can't stop me from taking a better-paid job. Mrs. Ludorf, if you really want to know, the cost of living has risen so much and the value of the pound is so much less than it was when I first came here, and my family's grown bigger too.'

'Who do you think will come in your place?' asked Mrs. Ludorf.

'There's been talk of that niece of Mrs. Kuhn's.'

'Fancy giving your job to a sixteen-year-old kid, fresh from school with no office experience at all. Forty-five pounds! And yet they can't give you that with your university education, and years of experience.' Mrs. Ludorf sounded quite indignant.

'But he can't take a person (a white one, that is) of my experience because he would have to pay her three times as much as he pays me. The excuse is always that our standard of living is lower,' I said wearily.

After a few minutes, she asked, 'Where does your husband work?'

'Braamfontein.'

'What kind of work does he do?'

'It's a clerical job; almost the same kind of work we do here. Keeping records for the college. I believe he's also a kind of personnel manager. For the black staff, I mean.'

She nodded.

'That's a good job. How long has he been with them?'

'Oh, he's been there ever since he left school. Over fifteen years now.'

'He must be Managing Director by now already, like Adam. Adam is the Managing Director here, isn't he?' she said, laughing.

Adam *was*, to all intents and purposes, the Managing Director of Metropolitan Radio, but his pay packet did not reflect the fact.

I had only to go to Continental Scooter Repairs for a week to get acclimatised to my new work. The work had been easy and I had no trouble learning it, so it became unnecessary for me to report every morning before starting at Metropolitan. But I had kept in contact with my prospective employer by telephone. The last time I had heard from him, he had reported to the Labour and Industrial Offices his intention to employ a non-white worker, and the inspector had informed him that he would call at the garage to see if conditions of work there were 'suitable'.

Two days before I was due to leave Metropolitan Radio and start the new job, I went to Gant's to phone. I put the five-cent piece in the slot and waited for someone to answer the telephone. It was my prospective employer himself.

'Hello, is that Muriel?'

'Yes, Mr. Saladino. Did the inspectors come?'

'Yes, they did, and I am very disappointed.'

'Why?' My heart began to beat faster.

'Because they tell me now I must build another toilet, you know. They say we can't use the same toilet because you are non-white.'

'But I can use the same toilet as your other black workers, the ones who work in your garage.'

"No, no, no. If they know I have a non-white girl here working for me, and I don't have a separate toilet for her, they'll charge me.'

'But I don't have a separate toilet here at Metropolitan and I have been working here for years and my employer has never been charged.'

'Yes but you do not know what they do to us immigrants. They look for excuses to get us out of business, you know. Your boss is a Jew, and they bribe these Boers, not to charge them.'

I asked unsteadily, 'Now what are we going to do?'

'Well, I'll call in a builder to see whether we can build a toilet. But they also said I can't use the same office as you, that I'll have to build a separate one for you. I *told* them, I'm in the workshop most of the time and not in the office.'

'But I have never had my own office, you know that!'

'I told you, Muriel. Your boss bribes the Boers. What can I do? I really want you to come and work for me but the law makes it impossible. They even say I have to have a change-room for you.'

'A change-room? What's that?' I cried.

'You see, Muriel, it is just impossible. If they come into this office and find me sitting with you, they'll start trouble, you know that. You understand, don't you?'

'Yes, I understand, Mr. Saladino.'

'I'm sorry, Muriel, honestly I'm sorry. I'm afraid you'll just have to wait. It may take months, I don't know. Anyway, I'll let you know … I'll keep in touch …'

I put the phone down. Impossible to describe the emotional conflict I was in as I walked back to Metropolitan Radio, moving like a mechanical thing. My mind was in a turmoil.

These damnable laws which dictate to you where, and next to whom, you shall walk, sit, stand and lie … This whole abominable nauseating business of toilets and 'separate but equal facilities' … What is one to do anyway? One is forever in a trap from which there is no way of escape … except suicide.

I crossed the road like a robot against the red light, with no presence of mind. The next moment, I was standing dead still in the middle of the road … From some distant place came the shrill screaming voice of a woman; and in a split second, a car squeaked to a precipitate jerky stop next to me, missing my tremulous numb form by a fraction of an inch.

Back at my desk, I made up my mind. I was no longer trembling and hesitant. I took a blank sheet of paper from my desk, and I scribbled my formal letter of resignation. Until then I had only given verbal notice. I decided to write the letter in my own handwriting instead of typing it. My hand just glided over the sheet. I looked at the letter just before I put it into the envelope. I remembered the resignation note I had once written, after so many false starts, wavering, uncertain, and compared it to that final one. My handwriting had never looked so beautiful. I had at last decided to free myself of the shackles which had bound not only my hands, but also my soul.

When I took my bag and said to the boss, 'Good night, Mr. Bloch' for the last time, I did not know what the future held in store for me. I did not care. I had no regrets. All I knew was that I could not continue to be part of the web that has been woven to entangle a people whom I love and am part of. I would never again place myself in a position in which I had to ask for pass-books or be 'loyal to the firm' at my own people's expense. My conscience would be clear.

And I added, as I looked into Mr. Bloch's eyes:
'Thanks for everything.'